UNDERSTANDING
Standards-Based
EDUCATION

UNDERSTANDING
Standards-Based
EDUCATION

A Practical Guide
for Teachers and
Administrators

Richard Zagranski
William T. Whigham
Patrice L. Dardenne

CORWIN PRESS
A SAGE Company
Thousand Oaks, CA 91320

For information:

Corwin Press
A SAGE Company
2455 Teller Road
Thousand Oaks, California 91320
www.corwinpress.com

SAGE India Pvt. Ltd.
B 1/I 1 Mohan Cooperative Industrial Area
Mathura Road, New Delhi 110 044
India

SAGE Ltd.
1 Oliver's Yard
55 City Road
London EC1Y 1SP
United Kingdom

SAGE Asia-Pacific Pte. Ltd.
33 Pekin Street #02–01
Far East Square
Singapore 048763

Printed in the United States of America

Library of Congress Cataloging-in-Publication Data

Zagranski, Richard.
Understanding standards-based education: a practical guide for teachers and administrators/Richard Zagranski, William T. Whigham, Patrice L. Dardenne.
    p. cm.
Includes bibliographical references and index.
ISBN 978-1-4129-5571-3 (cloth)
ISBN 978-1-4129-5572-0 (pbk.)
    1. Education—Standards—United States—Handbooks, manuals, etc.
2. Educational accountability—United States—Handbooks, manuals, etc.
3. Educational evaluation—United States—Handbooks, manuals, etc.
I. Whigham, William T. II. Dardenne, Patrice L. III. Title.

LB3060.83.Z34 2008
379.1′58—dc22   2007020990

This book is printed on acid-free paper.

07   08   09   10   10 9 8 7 6 5 4 3 2 1

Acquisitions Editor:	Carol Chambers Collins
Editorial Assistant:	Gem Rabanera
Production Editor:	Libby Larson
Copy Editor:	Trey Thoelcke
Typesetter:	C&M Digitals (P) Ltd.
Proofreader:	Theresa Kay
Indexer:	Rick Hurd
Graphic Designer:	Lisa Miller

Contents

List of Figures

Preface

A famous scientist said that the decade from 1950 to 1960 doubled the knowledge base that had previously been acquired since the beginning of recorded time. Since 1960, that knowledge base has continued to double with even more frequency. Technological development has occurred at such a rapid pace that school systems have struggled to keep up, always searching for meaningful instruction and not for faddish components that burn out quickly. Reinventing the modern school actually meant going back to the driving goal of standards-based education: what should a student know and be able to do, and how can an educator verify that the student can apply the skills successfully, repeatedly, and consistently in a variety of situations. Our premise is that "Education is the ability to do, not just the capacity to know." In that light, this book provides the tools and understandings that are necessary to make a difference. Everyone, from the administrator to the teacher, student, and parent, clearly understands the expectations and accountability to achieve the goal of quality education.

The book is laid out in user-friendly language and guides the readers through the steps of the standards-based process. The text provides examples and assessment pieces for all of the stakeholders to measure the levels of success and to provide an ongoing process of adjustment and revision. The text shows how to use the standards-based method to change learning from teacher input models to learner output ones. Using a Pyramid of Responsibility as a guide (identified in Chapter 1), everyone involved in the education process is held accountable for the learning.

ACKNOWLEDGMENTS

Corwin Press gratefully thanks the following peer-reviewers for their contributions to this book:

Dr. Vaughn Rhudy
Teacher
Shady Spring High School
Shady Spring, WV

John Scholten
Superintendent
Glen Lake Community Schools
Maple City, MI

Patricia Baker
Teacher, NBCT Middle Childhood Generalist
Mary Walter Elementary School
Bealeton, VA

Amanda Mayeaux
Teacher
Dutchtown Middle School
Geismat, LA

Russ Adams
Principal
MOC-Floyd Valley High
Orange City, IA

Erica Ann Faginski
Principal
Michael E. Smith Middle School
South Hadley, MA

About the Authors

 **Richard Zagranski** was a teacher for 40 years at South Hadley High School, South Hadley, Massachusetts. During that time he also held the following administrative positions: English Department Chairman, District Curriculum Coordinator for English, Chairman of the Teacher Evaluation Committee, Chairman of the Reaccreditation Committee, and Chairman of the Philosophy and Objectives Committee. In addition, he has been an Adjunct Instructor at both Holyoke Community College and at Fitchburg State College, both in Massachusetts. Currently, he is a standards-based consultant working with school systems in and around the New England area. The information and techniques presented in this guide are field-tested approaches, which he has refined through research and trial and error.

 **William T. Whigham** has been a teacher for more than 30 years in both middle and high schools, during which time he has served as an Interim Assistant Principal, Cochairman of the District Curriculum Committee, Grants Manager, Director of Physical Education and Athletics, Adjunct Instructor for Student Teachers at Springfield College, Adjunct Instructor at Fitchburg State College, and standards-based consultant. He is the author of the first No Child Left Behind implementation program used by the South Hadley, Massachusetts, school system. He is currently working with Springfield College, Springfield, Massachusetts, in the future teachers program, bringing in accountability and assessment standards. Likewise, he serves as a standards-based consultant in the New England region.

 **Patrice L. Dardenne** has been involved in education for more than 30 years, during which time he has served as Assistant Superintendent for Accountability (responsible for the development, implementation, and operation of the school system's assessment systems, data management systems, NCLB grant program, curriculum, and technology initiatives), Interim Superintendent, Assistant to the Superintendent for Management Services (including professional development programs for the staff), Adjunct

Instructor at American International College, Director of Special Education, and Dean of Students/Guidance Counselor. Likewise he has served as an evaluation consultant and an educational software consultant in Monterey, California, working with the school district to institute assessment and data management services. He was recently appointed to the position of Superintendent of Schools in Hatfield, Massachusetts.

This book is dedicated to Marlene, Kristen, Richard M., Al, and Julia Zagranski for their continued love and support, and to Jen Koch for keeping me mentally and physically nourished; to Connie Whigham and Tonya Walker for their loyalty and encouragement in helping to bring this project to fruition; and to Roxanne and Caitlin Dardenne for their confidence and trust that we were doing something beneficial for others.

Introduction 1

For years, educational leaders, teachers, and parents have struggled with one question: What should the schools be teaching? Everyone had a theory and an opinion, which were generally shaped by the needs of the moment. As society went through cyclic changes (hippies, yuppies, and so on), school systems were urged to try to meet the needs of the present generation (open campus, new math, linguistics, and the like).

In recent years, however, educational districts and legislatures across the country have stopped the merry-go-round process of change for change's sake in order to examine content and methods more closely using current scientific research to give validity to their scrutiny. The overall consensus they reached was that state standards, founded on a solid content base of essential knowledge, were necessary as a bedrock for learning for all students. The skills required in a global marketplace were identified, and a process for obtaining and solidifying these skills was undertaken by state governments in conjunction with recognized educational leaders. Second, students were no longer going to be asked to compete against their peers to see who was on which rung of the achievement ladder; instead, they would be working to establish their own rate of accomplishment and success in mastering these core concepts. Enrichment would still be there, but first students had to have the necessary foundation.

RELEVANT VERSUS RELATIVE

Two terms became essential in the education vocabulary: *relevant* and *relative*. Relevant knowledge and skills were those essential for all students to know and be able to do (such as adding a column of figures, using punctuation in a sentence, and identifying patterns). Relative knowledge consists of whatever fits into the "nice but not essential to know" category. The word *zephyr* is a good example of relative knowledge because it's a word that's often included in many high school vocabulary books, most likely added just to satisfy some desire for a word beginning with each letter of the alphabet. While knowing the definition is "nice," one rarely, if ever, finds the word in daily usage. Most people have probably spent productive lives without ever encountering the word. Yet the word *zephyr* is rarely differentiated from words that are essential to know.

In short, a system was needed to make sure that relevant knowledge was taught and learned first so that students had a strong base upon which to build. That premise became the reason for the establishment of state standards and the No Child Left Behind Act of 2002.

THE PROBLEMS

The first problem is that most teachers, many students, and almost all parents have been taught using the old, traditional method, which often made no distinction between relevant and relative knowledge and skills. Second, traditional classrooms pitted students against each other, forcing them to compete for the top spot and even offering incentives. Teachers would scale grades as a way to pass students who really hadn't mastered core knowledge and skills. Although some students received the relevant knowledge base and were able to progress well into enrichment, others received an unsteady foundation of relevant and relative knowledge, which actually created confusion and uncertainty. Since the curriculum was imprecise and usually overloaded, teachers often ran out of time trying to cover more material than was necessary, and yet they still felt compelled to move on to the next topic.

To make matters worse, the curriculum itself was usually a document produced mainly to satisfy reaccreditation committees. In reality, the curriculum was neither consistent nor was its specific use actively enforced. Teachers, however, felt strangely obligated to complete as much of it as possible, primarily because they weren't sure what part of the curriculum was essential to teach. Think about the times in your own school experience that you took a test or quiz, did poorly, and never had a chance to learn why you were wrong in your answers. The next day, ready or not, the class began another topic. Since the teacher couldn't stop, this meant that you either had to catch up on your own or you were left behind. What about the students that had difficulty in acquiring the essential base of knowledge? With nowhere to turn, they became frustrated by their lack of success and essentially either went through the motions of learning or rationalized their own failure by shutting down on the whole education process.

Teachers also experienced problems since, in many cases, they had developed traditional lessons that they enjoyed teaching because they had developed an expertise in these areas. The fact that some of these lessons were just "nice to know," and didn't build the foundation necessary for students to understand them or apply what they had learned, really didn't make any difference. Teachers lived by the motto, "If it isn't broken, then don't fix it." At the same time, many of these teachers used their tests only to "get a grade" so they'd have something to put into the grade book to indicate some type of differentiation among students rather than to track students' progress and make adjustments.

While this process was going on, most parents, who'd likely been taught using the "shotgun curriculum" method (if you shoot out enough pellets of knowledge, some might hit the target), were confused by what their children were supposed to be learning. They didn't understand that "less is more." Even worse, they couldn't comprehend that organizing a strong core base of essential knowledge may mean removing some elements of instruction now, in order to introduce them later when the proper foundation has been laid and the time is optimal. Because much of the parents' educational motivation from their own parents had been based on "why aren't you doing as well as Jimmy," present-day parents really weren't quite sure what to do when "Jimmy" was removed from the picture. Although they now had to deal with their own child's ability to achieve and to develop mastery, they didn't know where to start.

THE SOLUTION

Whether you're a student, parent, teacher, principal, superintendent, or someone in between, you need to ask only two questions: "Where do I start?" and "What do I need to know?" To answer these questions, this workbook was designed in pyramidal form to emphasize the need for a strong base, which acts as a foundation of support for all of the material piled on top. Likewise, this format is devised to demonstrate clearly the ascending levels of accountability that develop in a standards-based system. In an effort to ensure that everyone's roles and responsibilities are distinctly defined, the contents are structured around three basic statements: *what everyone needs to know, what most people need to know,* and *what some people need to know.* These three statements are then molded into a working pyramid (see Figure 1.1).

Figure 1.1   Pyramid of Responsibility

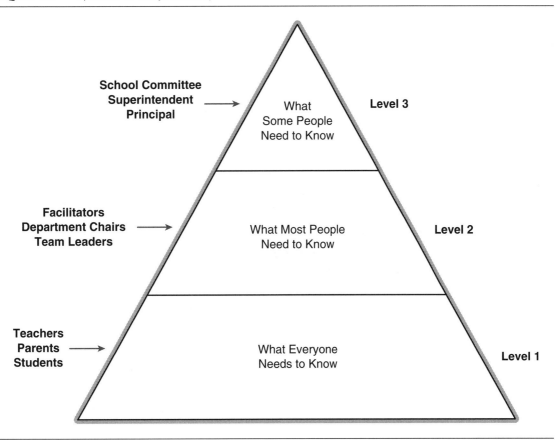

In order to use this book, simply determine into which category you belong, then learn everything that your category "needs to know." As the pyramid illustrates, the higher the designation, the more information you'll be responsible for learning.

Level 3 corresponds to the upper echelon of administration: school committees, superintendents, and principals. Because these people are educational leaders and communicators who formulate and enact decisions that keep the school community active, informed, and on-track, they are at the apex of the system and must possess all of the information covered in the entire pyramid. Their focus is on district planning, hiring, evaluation, funding, coordination, standards assurance, and so on.

Curriculum facilitators, grade-level coordinators, team leaders, department chairs, vice principals, and all middle administrators fall under Level 2. While it's nice for them to have a grasp on what happens at the level above them so that they can provide data and insight to help shape the direction of the district, their main focus is on the middle and lower levels of the pyramid. By fully understanding these two areas, they can better provide support, leadership, mentoring, and accountability to those people below them, while ensuring that the teachers have the facilities, materials, and training to keep students moving toward the established goals. They also often act as a conduit of information between the parent and the teacher.

Level 1, or the base of the pyramid, is the foundation segment that the teachers need to know. It's the area that contains all of the information they need to accomplish their primary goal of providing standards-based instruction to students, as well as their secondary objective of creating enrichment opportunities once the students have mastered the core knowledge. Although teachers should be aware of the other levels of knowledge, since teachers provide the individual pieces of data that go into the composite profile of the district, they are technically responsible only for ensuring that the pertinent information is collected at their level and is transmitted to the proper destination (Level 2). The data is then used to diagnose overall areas of concern, strengthen positive programs, and verify the degree of success or failure of an individual area. Parents and students also fit into this level because they must be acutely aware of the standards, as well as the methods of classroom instruction being provided to meet the standards. Furthermore, since they are the most important stakeholders, parents and students also share in the responsibility for ensuring the program's success.

CONTENT AND INTENT

This workbook is organized in a format that highlights the responsibilities of each of the three groups (Levels 1, 2, and 3) in regard to their main areas of concern, and is written so that each group knows where its primary focus of attention should be directed. For example: Teacher A should concentrate on the information in Level 1, be aware of the basics in Level 2, and not be totally occupied with the responsibilities of Level 3. On the other hand, Facilitator B needs to thoroughly understand Levels 1 and 2 while maintaining a working knowledge of Level 3. Finally, Superintendent C must master Levels 1 to 3, and not only is required to know that job but also the obligations of Facilitator B and Teacher A. To assist with this process, the following content is supplied throughout the text:

- Templates
- Rubrics
- Checklists
- Model lessons
- Teacher and parent aids

Now, with all of this content, one might expect a complicated theory-based presentation. But the important goal of this text is simple: to present a method of standards-based education that works, based on the requirements for what a student should know and be able to do (the standards).

Instead of addressing complex theories that often have no direct relationship to real-world teaching practices, the focus of this workbook is on what each group of educators is expected to accomplish or know in order to assure success in a standards-based classroom. In an effort to meet these needs, this book provides teachers with the information, tools, and support necessary for them to keep their lessons centered on recognized standards of performance and assessment. But the usefulness doesn't stop there. The book also delivers a wealth of information to students and parents so they can gain a meaningful understanding of the standards-based process and be better prepared to interact with teachers toward mutually shared goals. Behind this attention to parents and students is the belief that the more they know about the way lessons are structured, how performance objectives are designed, and how assessments are administered, the more active students and parents can be in forming a community of learning. Therefore, along with everything else, some of the chapters contain specific tools for parents to use to make sure they can properly assess the needs of their children in order to provide help and support.

2 Traditional Versus Standards-Based Education

Although standards-based education has been around for a number of years, not everyone clearly understands how it differs from the traditional system. In many cases, information has dribbled out, often incomplete, sometimes misleading. Much emphasis has been placed on state or national testing practices, as these provide a sensationalism that the media can run with, but little is written on what happens in the classroom between teacher and student. Parents, especially, have received inadequate or imprecise information. This lack of a clear understanding has kept some people wondering and wavering in their commitment to what they perceive to be nothing but more of the same. Their argument often hinges on "but I learned in the traditional way, and look how well I turned out." However, the standards-based model is different because it creates a shift in the paradigm—the focus is on what students learn rather than on what teachers teach.

For many years, traditional schools have operated in the type of sequence seen in Figure 2.1.

Curriculum becomes the magic word, the driving force; everything hinges on the successful completion of the curriculum. There is a rush to make sure that everyone has a curriculum, is on the same page with the curriculum, and completes everything the curriculum demands. But, in reality, what is the curriculum? How many schools have actually defined the term for their teachers or, more precisely, dissected the word into its component parts? *Curriculum* is actually defined by *The New American Heritage Dictionary of the English Language* as "all the courses of study offered by an institution." That is a broad statement, which seems to indicate that instructional strategies and assessment are also a part of curriculum. *Curriculum* is a broad term that actually encompasses all that a "teacher is supposed to do."

Without breaking the term into understandable pieces, traditional schools approach curriculum by how many books, chapters, pages, worksheets, and

Curriculum is beyond "stuff that lasts Friday"

6

Figure 2.1   Drivetrain Sequence of the Traditional School

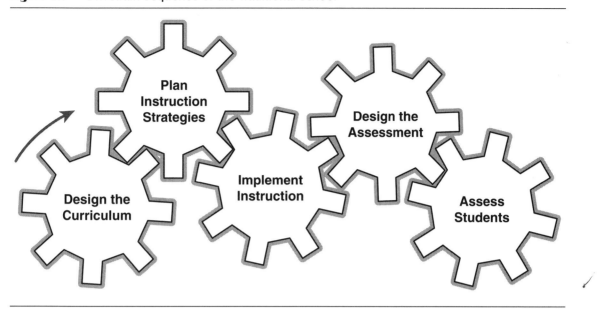

the like have to be covered in a given amount of time, generally a school year. The danger is in equating numbers of pages and chapters covered to the degree of learning that is desired. Traditional schools design the curriculum (which often consists of page numbers tied to lessons from texts) and then plan instructional activities. After this, they provide the instruction. Then they design the assessment and, finally, assess the students. Many times, the assessment becomes simply a grade in a book, and not a tool to adjust learning. Because the curriculum is often open-ended, there is little time to review and reexamine areas of difficulty. While this system may appear to work (since most current educators were raised in it), it has numerous flaws. Foremost is how to select texts, plan units, and design lessons without knowing what the learning goals are; only by looking at what you want to assess will you know what you specifically want to achieve. Therefore, you really must look at the expected end result before you design the steps to get there. Remember, traditional schools emphasized teaching; standards-based ones focus on learning.

WHAT EVERYONE NEEDS TO KNOW

To get a clearer picture of the differences between traditional and standards-based schools, one has to look only at their underlying characteristics.

Characteristics of traditional schools all too often include the following.

- In designing the curriculum without the assessment, the schools often provide more relative than relevant material; students struggle to find patterns or meaning from the instruction.

- Students often are unaware of their performance level until it is too late to make adequate corrections.

- If students are unclear about the expectations, their performance and their behavior often suffer.

- Teachers have a difficult time ensuring that all students receive the standards required for successful transition to the next grade because the curriculum is not specific enough about learning objectives.

- Teachers are hard pressed to cover all of the material presented in the curriculum due to a lack of time.

Designing the curriculum first is like packing to go on a mystery vacation. Will the weather be cold or hot? Rainy or dry? Will you be near the ocean or the mountains? Mostly indoors or outside? You pack for all occasions, so you end up using only a few of the items you bring along. But, you always want to make sure you have enough. The same goes for designing a curriculum without knowing specifically what you wish to accomplish. Educators overpack and then face the risk of spending too much time covering too many crammed-together items at the beginning of the year and running out of time to get to the remainder of the contents of the educational suitcase near the end of the year. Many students know more about the Revolutionary War and the geography of North America before 1834 than they do about current events and the geography of the present. Maybe it's because teachers spend a tremendous amount of "curriculum" time on that early period, then run out of time before reaching the twenty-first century.

Attempting to design a curriculum without the end goal has unfortunate consequences.

- Quantity of material overwhelms quality of learning.
- Time becomes an enemy rather than an ally in the learning process with teachers finding themselves saying, "but we've got to move on" or "we still have a lot of material to cover."
- Students have insufficient time for processing, reflection, and application.
- Assessment often becomes a system for justifying grades rather than for making sure that learning takes place.
- No built-in process for evaluating and refining the drivetrain exists; the "curriculum" becomes locked in place. Teachers pick and choose those elements they feel comfortable with, and all too often focus their attention on the teacher's level of interest or expertise rather than on the standards.
- Schools become locked into texts or kits that look nice but do not cover all of the standards. Because of the investment in them, teachers either find themselves saddled with a scope and sequence that is incomplete, or they simply ignore the text and fend for themselves and their students, hoping to find materials that will allow the class to succeed.

So you set out on the mystery vacation trip, not knowing where you are going or how you are going to know when you get there. You have a bunch of maps and books all touting the numerous attractions, but you really can't plan since you continually have to sort out what you are doing from what you feel you should be doing. Think of the movie *National Lampoon's Vacation,* in which the family, trying to reach Wally World, is sidetracked by the lure of the world's largest ball of string or the house of mud. Are these attractions important enough to provide some vital bit of life-altering knowledge or skill that shouldn't be missed? Without a plan of action, you have a tendency to visit many places that are unnecessary. You'll create a false need. You'll have difficulty budgeting time. Likewise, with no evaluation of the process, you can't tell your friends how to make the journey more efficient if they wish to undertake the trip. You'll have a tendency to complain but not to offer alternative solutions. Your assessment, if you make one, will be of the entire trip and not of the component parts.

The experience is much like making up a test or quiz after a unit of study, administering it, finding out that some children didn't pass, but still having to move on to the next unit. Why? The answer lies mainly in the fact that the curriculum is so vague and so broad that many teachers are unaware of when they have covered all of the material they are required to cover. Likewise, they aren't always clear about determining if the students have really learned and can use what they have been taught. Even if they discover that not everyone in the class "got it," what can they do but move on and hope the slower achieving students will catch up? The curriculum is often jammed with content that the teacher has to sort out. Older textbooks are not often sequenced with the standards in mind. With budget cuts facing many school systems and with rising costs of new texts, many schools are saddled with having to do with what they already have. Quantity is constantly being weighed against quality. The temptation is to keep the status quo and ride out the standards-based movement, but that is folly since this movement is here to stay . . . with teeth.

Figure 2.2 illustrates the design of the standards-based model, which places assessment and establishment of performance levels prior to designing the curriculum.

Notice the differences in the process of the standards-based school (see Figure 2.2). The most obvious variation is that one does not begin to design the curriculum until other pieces have been put into place and have been addressed. A beginning and an endpoint are established before texts, chapters, and problems are used to support the learning. Teachers know exactly what they have to teach and are then more aware of which supplementary materials best help them to complete the job. The curriculum plugs into the standards. In this way, the approach ensures that every student covers all of the relevant learning and then has the knowledge to apply what has been learned into real-world problem-solving settings.

- The content standards are written first so the teacher doesn't have to guess what specifics or basics each student is expected to know.

- The assessment comes next in order to create a clear target for what students are supposed to know and be able to do.

Figure 2.2   Drivetrain Sequence of the Standards-Based School

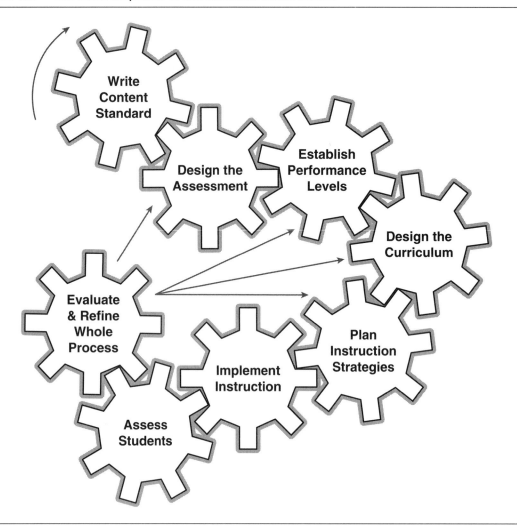

- The students know precisely what is expected of them; they can, in an ongoing manner, monitor and adjust their performances.

- The assessments are prescriptive and not just driven by grades.

- Students are more responsible for their own learning since they receive ongoing feedback, and the teacher can check for understanding.

- Tests are performance indicators and not punitive instruments.

- The curriculum is designed to match the content standards; there are no gaps between the standards and the curriculum.

- The teacher, knowing what is to be taught, can then plan the instructional strategies necessary to achieve the desired result.

- The process has a built-in and ongoing evaluation; adjustments are constantly being made.

- While the standards may remain consistent, supplementary materials (such as texts) can be updated regularly.

- Teachers use data to adjust student learning.

- Homework has relevance and is not used as busywork, a quick grade, a requirement because "parents expect homework," or as a punitive measure.

- The focus is on what students have learned rather than what teachers have covered.

- Parents are constantly informed of student progress; they are used as resources rather than as adversaries.

- Teachers begin to think in terms of assessments rather than just in grades.

- The teacher is more in control of time; students are better able to progress at a pace that is most conducive to their individual learning style.

- The standards apply to *all* students.

- Once students understand the standards, they then can do enrichment activities.

WHAT MOST PEOPLE NEED TO KNOW

Although the basic principles of standards-based education are logical and sound, one shouldn't jump to the conclusion that an educator can do a complete about-face from the traditional approach to the standards-based one immediately. Remember, most administrators, teachers, and parents have been trained in the traditional approach. There must be a rethinking as well as a relearning to make the transition smooth. A great deal of work needs to be done, involving teacher training, professional development, and supervision, in order to make the transition successful.

- Newly graduated teachers need to be introduced to the standards-based model immediately.

- Most long-time faculty have been taught using the traditional model, so self-assessment of where they are in the standards-based approach is essential.

- Long-term, sustained professional development is vitally important in providing these experienced teachers with the essentials necessary for them to succeed.
  - Development objectives must be clearly outlined, and a timetable for improvement needs to be established with each teacher.
  - Teachers should receive immediate feedback on their attempts to use the elements of the standards-based model in their instruction.

- Standards that the students are working on should be plainly posted in the classroom in a language conducive to the grade level.

- Teachers need to show the relevance of the standards to each lesson, assignment, project, and assessment.

- Performance objectives need to be established across the board, with all teachers and students responsible to achieve these same objectives.

- Faculty and/or department meetings should regularly address some aspect of standards-based learning.

- Teachers need to be instructed on the gathering, as well as the use, of data. They must become proficient at using classroom, district, state, and national data to make instructional decisions and create strategies to increase learning.

- Teachers should be provided with support: observations of teachers successfully using the standards-based model, a mentor teacher if possible, instruction in areas of weakness, and so on.

- All textbooks and supplementary materials should be examined in light of standards-based instruction, and a replacement plan of action must be developed to deal with major inconsistencies.

- Sufficient materials should be made available to all grade-level teachers.

- New materials should be reviewed in light of their applicability to a standards-based model.

- School/district budgets should include professional development monies to provide teachers with ongoing opportunities for instruction and observation.

Change from the traditional curriculum, with all of its twists and turns, to a more concrete standards-based model requires a commitment throughout the chain of command. Just telling teachers to "do it" or parents to "accept it" is probably the worst way to introduce standards-based education into a community. Thoughtful preparation, a clearly defined process, input from all of the stakeholders, and an understanding that all of this is not meant just to pass a state standardized test are all vital ingredients in successful implementation. Recognizing that teacher creativity is enhanced since educators can focus on lesson delivery rather than on knowledge creation is a key component.

WHAT SOME PEOPLE NEED TO KNOW

Administrators need to be proactive and visible in the schools and in the classrooms. They need to set the tone and provide the motivation to implement standards-based education, all the time, for all the students. The checklist in Figure 2.3 is provided for administrators so they may look at policies and procedures they are presently using to make sure they focus on standards-based instruction.

Accountability for implementation, as well as for monitoring and adjustments, will be high on the priority scale. Administrators will need to be hands-on people who are visible more in the classrooms than in school committee rooms.

Figure 2.3   Administration Checklist

AREAS TO BE ADDRESSED	YES	NO	SOLUTIONS
Both new teachers and veteran staff are required to demonstrate content proficiency as a condition of employment.			
Content review sessions are frequently offered for teachers after school, in college extension courses, or during summers.			
Teachers are provided with a "needs assessment" form; the data obtained is coordinated with student performance assessment data and is used to provide the basis for professional development.			
Professional development days for teachers and middle managers (full days, half days, or hours) are built into the school calendar.			
Professional development days and offerings are structured around student learning and not around clerical matters.			
Teachers who attend outside professional development programs are required to report on them and share information at grade-level, department, or faculty meetings.			
Outside professional development activities pursued by teachers must be aligned with the district mission and goals.			
Teaching materials are reviewed, replaced, and updated on a predetermined schedule.			
All new staff receive an initial orientation session, as well as monthly updates, during which they can ask questions and share concerns.			
All new teachers are provided with a mentor teacher (for an entire year) who is versed in standards-based education.			
A portion of each grade-level, department, or faculty meeting is set aside to discuss or present information, strategies, lessons, and so on, involving standards-based teaching.			
Teachers are encouraged to post lessons and units on the Web.			

HOW DO WE GET THERE FROM HERE?

A teacher can best build a community of learning (whether that be a single teacher-student-parent arrangement or a classroom full of them) in the following ways.

- Become informed about the differences between the traditional and standards-based approaches to education.
- Do a self-assessment to determine where you fall in the spectrum: hard-core traditionalist, moderate traditionalist willing to listen, using some standards-based instruction, running a standards-based classroom.
- Based on your results, seek instruction through professional development programs, workshops, speakers, peer teachers, curriculum committees, or administrators.
- Work with colleagues to increase understanding, pilot and share lessons, create assessments, analyze data, and adjust teaching strategies.
- Use a self-assessment rubric (see Figure 8.4 in Chapter 8) to calculate progress.
- Develop a communication system (a brief objective sheet to be sent out to parents weekly or monthly) to increase awareness.
- Urge the administration to provide parent information sessions involving standards-based education through the use of general meetings, Web sites, media, brochures, newspaper articles, mailings, and so on.

QUESTIONS FOR REFLECTION

Traditionally, teachers have received calls from parents all focused on "How come . . . ?"

- "How come my daughter was getting an A last year, but now she's getting only a C?"
- "How come my son didn't get Teacher A; that class is two chapters ahead."
- "How come Teacher B doesn't give any homework?"
- "How come my son has to read this text when Teacher C's students don't?"
- "How come Jane has to do an extra composition when Jack doesn't?"

There are endless "How come?" questions that all lend themselves to the traditional curriculum with its unclear goals, objectives, and assessments. Once parents begin to understand the aims of standard-based education, then the questions change; the inquiries become more focused on helping the students to learn:

- "What standards is the teacher covering today?"
- "How will the students know when they have mastered the standards?"

- "How is my child progressing toward mastery of the standards?"
- "What enrichment opportunities are provided once my child masters the standards?"
- "How can I help my child to succeed?"

These questions have much clearer answers under a standards-based system because the parents know in the beginning what the teacher is attempting to achieve and can help to work toward the goal.

SUMMARY

The best way to summarize this chapter is to look at what a traditional system contains and what a standards-based system produces. This is the same type of focus that separates an educational system that concentrates on teaching from one that stresses learning.

A traditional curriculum system generally looks like the following:

- A traditional curriculum is in place and often provides more related than relevant knowledge.
- An assessment, which is often an afterthought and which may be based on the need for a grade rather than used as an indicator of learning, is a limiting factor.
- Standards are plugged into the preexisting curriculum, which may result in certain standards being overlooked or not addressed.
- Opportunities to correct and adjust learning may be diminished due to the need to reach an unclearly defined end point.
- Performance objectives and assessments are variable among teachers in the same grade level.

A standards-based system produces the following:

- Students know up front what the performance objectives and assessment are.
- Teachers, knowing what they have to achieve, can have a better control of time to promote learning.
- The focus is on what students need to learn rather than on what teachers want to teach.
- Students are held more accountable for their own learning, since they are in competition with themselves and not with their peers.
- Students can better monitor their progress, and so have opportunities to make corrections and adjustments.

3 Accountability

During the reign of King Arthur, his knights represented the different fiefdoms throughout the newly organized Britain. Before Arthur, these men had lived independently in mini-principalities within the borders of a single country. Independent rulers, mini-kings, each made laws, exacted penalties, and collected taxes. Arthur provided these kings a reason to come together under one rule, to break up the little monarchies and join one big one with a definitive leader. This form of rule offered benefits: fewer wars against each other, a standard set of laws and punishments, and a chance to be united against common enemies. But, while the mini-kings were willing to absorb the benefits, they were reluctant to give up their autonomy completely. Instead, their fiefdoms were only partially accountable to Arthur.

Traditional schools have been constructed much like a series of fiefdoms under a single ruler, the principal. The teachers operate in their "isolated castles" or classrooms, often in little contact with their colleagues next door. They each receive the same rules and policies, and they each attend "court" in faculty meetings. However, their level of accountability often differs (if it didn't, there would be no real need for the number of faculty meetings that dwell on teamwork, uniformity of standards, enforcement of discipline codes, morale, curriculum coordination, and the myriad of other issues that constantly need reinforcement). Some teachers go precisely by the book, handing out discipline and rewards to the extent prescribed by the student handbook. They stick to the curriculum exactly, give the same tests and assignments year after year, and can be counted on to be doing the same lesson on this date next year, the year after, and so on. They have a timetable that indicates where they should be in relationship to the material being covered, not where the students need to be. Other teachers follow the discipline and reward code they feel should be in effect, not necessarily the one determined by the faculty committees and administration. They change the curriculum to meet their needs and student interests, cover the standards to some degree or other, give different tests depending on what they choose to use as a text, and spend a disproportionate amount of time on lessons or topics they especially enjoy, regardless of their relevancy.

In both cases, there is little sharing of ideas or educational strategies. Both of these are teacher input systems in which the teacher does the teaching and the student supposedly absorbs the learning. Fortunately, most teachers aren't comfortable with either system. They recognize that a school's purpose is for student learning to occur, and that a school is not just a place where teachers stand in front of a class and present information, regardless of the outcome.

RAISE THE DRAWBRIDGE, FLOOD THE MOAT

Once the traditional teachers enter their classes, they shut the door (which is equivalent to pulling up the drawbridge) and become the rulers of their mini-kingdoms. Those four walls serve as much to keep the students in as to keep other people out. They administer their own brand of teaching, sometimes but not always using the data from tests, quizzes, writings, and problem-solving exercises to alter in-class decision making about students. Something in the core nature of these teachers responds to one of two primitive urges: nobody ever told me how to do this job better; and I've used this strategy before, it seemed to work then, so I'll use it again even though the people and conditions have changed.

SURPRISE, SURPRISE, SURPRISE!

Now, one might think that most teachers would welcome the traditional approach, with its anonymity and its drawbridge mentality, but they really don't. The vast majority of teachers are conscientious people who truly want to do the best job possible for the students. Most of them recognize their own strengths and weaknesses, and want to get better. They welcome accountability because it provides them with feedback and consistency; the real teacher never stops being a learner and wants the information and training to continue to improve. They want the drawbridges down and the doors open to colleagues so they can share knowledge and strategies. They want the time with their peers to be able to discuss and focus on educational issues. They want the system to turn from teacher input to student output to provide data on whether and to what extent learning is taking place. As the knights of old discovered very quickly, working for one king that encompassed the whole land rather than for one ruler who controlled only a small part of the territory made more sense and produced more opportunities for success.

Smart teachers know that they aren't the creators of knowledge; that wasn't their function when they became teachers. They are the purveyors of knowledge, so they are involved in the strategies used to present this knowledge in a meaningful way to learners—and to make sure the learners "get it." But the teachers need outside sources to provide data that tells when and how the learners "get it." They need an accountability system that tells them whether what they do is successful; they need immediate feedback so they can revise and adjust while the opportunity to do so could still affect the learners.

The problem has often been that accountability was spotty, used only when a divisive or negative issue was raised, but not used often enough to promote positive learning. Accountability seemed to be more in evidence involving student absences or incidents of misbehavior than in learning a skill or a core of knowledge. There was always a strict record-keeping procedure used to count "tardies" and skipped classes, but one that compiled data on student learning was often lacking or incomplete. Accountability always seemed to revolve around a single isolated issue, but not on the need for a data system that could foster revision and change, if necessary. The accountability might exist between the teacher and students in a classroom, but it generally stopped there. And when data from the classroom was sent out, often the results were either slow in coming back, didn't come back at all, or came back in a format that was confusing or impossible to use. Administrators were often deluged with "administrivia," mundane tasks that tied them up and removed them from enough interaction with the total educational process and not just with discipline. They could not assist with data distribution and individual training, so results just piled up. Budgetary considerations often cut the position of the individual who was accountable to compile the data and make it available to the teachers and students in a usable format.

One department head, in cleaning out a classroom closet the summer after a teacher retired, discovered boxes of tests, quizzes, and writing samples stacked from floor to ceiling. All work had been carefully graded but with no commentary on any of the papers. There were no rubrics attached to indicate any standardization of performance levels. The boxes were arranged by year. Here were grades that were probably meticulously recorded in a grade book by date and assignment; the results were then translated into a report card mark, which may or may not have had relevance to the actual level of performance that the student had attained in class. This potential pile of data was then boxed and stored, apparently awaiting some future day of discovery. Obviously the teacher hadn't used it to drive decision making; the students did not have access to it once they had completed it; the system didn't have it to assess that learning across grade levels was taking place; and the teacher's colleagues on the next grade level up didn't have it to determine a student's prior knowledge. Like the stack of cut wood moldering in the swamp in Robert Frost's poem, "The Woodpile," a lot of work was potentially wasted.

Obviously the department chair understood that his discovery was also a reflection on him. Somehow he hadn't communicated to the teacher how important this data was, not by being saved in bulk to be burned in the school's furnace for a few degrees of heat, but to be used as exemplars and pieces of meaningful data on students and their accomplishments, as well as their needs. Somewhere in those boxes there was something that each teacher could have used to determine why the student in the next year of schooling was having difficulty.

ACCOUNTABILITY 101

The focus of this chapter is on the accountability of the teacher to the system of standards-based education, the student to the teacher, the student and teacher to the learning, and the parent to the standards-based process. While these are not the only agents involved in the learning pyramid, they are the principal stakeholders with an impact directly upon each other.

For the purpose of the pyramidal approach, educational accountability is defined as being answerable, responsible, and liable for the occurrence of learning.

Answerable for a teacher means having a reason and data to justify the learning procedures going on in and outside of the classroom. Basically, in a standards-based system, this means teaching to the standards, using the data from assessment pieces to revise and adjust, and justifying that everything in the class is relevant learning. Answerable for a student means accepting the role of a learner whose goal is to expand the skill base to a mastery level by self-challenge. For a parent it means becoming involved in the student's learning by being aware of the standards-based process, interacting with the student to reinforce the learning, and advocating for high levels of performance in positive ways.

Responsible means using feedback to revise and adjust the learning that is taking place. Through the use of short-term feedback, the teacher can provide scaffolding and differentiation to individual students in order to promote educational growth for all learners. Through long-term, skill-specific feedback, the teacher, working with the grade-level coordinators, can continue to monitor and modify the learning. The student is responsible for understanding that the standards-based system revolves around a growth process that allows time to learn from and correct errors.

Liable means contractually accountable to perform the duties as outlined in the job description, as well as by the educational system. For the teacher, this means using the standards-based format and the assessments contained within it to obtain the data to drive learning decisions in the classroom and throughout the district. Neither the student nor the parent is contractually bound to the educational system except by law in ensuring attendance. However, since the parent and student are the major benefactors and have such a high stake in the outcome, their commitment to performing the requirements inherent in a standards-based process should be of the highest priority.

WHAT EVERYONE NEEDS TO KNOW

One of the vital stakeholders in the accountability picture is the teacher, who has the immediate responsibility of dealing with the student on a day-to-day basis. The teacher's role in the accountability chain is extremely important, and is primarily to do the following.

- Develop a data collection tool to measure what students know and can do.
- Analyze and interpret data to drive classroom decision making.
- Share data to drive grade-level and district decision making.
- Create a student-centered learning environment.
- Increase student involvement and personal accountability in the education process.
- Increase parent involvement in both the education process and the accountability for results.
- Increase both cross grade-level as well as through grade-level coordination and information sharing with colleagues.

The teacher is accountable for providing and maintaining a standards-based learning environment in the classroom. To do this, a series of guidelines need to be established. Before teachers make decisions involving education, they must have a clearly defined goal. They have to think through what is essential for students to learn and be able to do.

Teachers not only have to be aware of what standards-based education is, but also how to apply the elements in the classroom. The shift from a teacher-centered environment (look, I'm teaching) to one that is student-centered (look, they're learning) must be thought through and adopted completely. To increase accountability, the teacher has to welcome observation and feedback from administrators, peers, and students. The teacher must become a master of content and strategy, and the teacher must be able to apply the content knowledge in problem-solving situations.

The checklist in Figure 3.1 is a tool for teacher self-examination to establish or identify his or her position in the accountability process. Multiple NO checkmarks in any area signal that the teacher needs reinforcement or additional training, while multiple YES marks demonstrate that the teacher is comfortable in that area.

The student is the reason the whole, complex educational system exists. Buildings, administrators, teachers, aides, educational researchers, support groups, textbook publishers, and even school bus manufacturers exist solely because the student does. An entire industry is centered on the success of this individual known as the student; therefore, there is an inherent obligation on the part of this learner to be a responsible consumer of education. There is an accountability factor that says the student must be serious about learning, must take advantage of all opportunities to excel, and must be willing to share the new skills and knowledge back with the investors, the community. In that regard, everyone has to know that the student is the most important person on the accountability list, and that the student is accountable for the following:

- Maintaining good attendance
- Being punctual
- Respecting the property of others
- Participating in a positive manner
- Respecting the rights of others
- Maintaining appropriate behavior
- Being prepared
- Resolving conflicts peacefully, using mediation when necessary
- Following school rules
- Performing at the highest individual level possible
- Dressing properly
- Discussing problems to find solutions
- Communicating with parents and teachers in a positive manner

Figure 3.1   Professional Accountability Checklist

ACCOUNTABILITY	YES	NO
I can explain different ways to problem-solve solutions in the specific content area.		
I encourage students to ask questions because I feel I have the content knowledge to answer them.		
I can provide and explain examples in the content area to assist student learning.		
I can design real-world learning application projects for the students.		
I use, understand, and can explain the terminology of the subject area.		
I would be comfortable discussing the content with peer teachers.		
I can communicate the content clearly in either a written or verbal manner.		
I can identify the skills the students need to use the content base correctly.		
I can arrive at the correct answers to problems in the text and on standards-based tests without using an answer key.		
STANDARDS-BASED CRITERIA	YES	NO
I understand and can design performance objectives.		
I understand, can create, and can explain the use of a variety of performance assessments.		
I understand, use, and can explain standards-based terminology.		
I understand how to tie the classroom learning into the real world.		
I understand, design, and use differentiation strategies.		
I understand, design, and use scaffolding strategies.		
I understand and can explain the differences in student learning styles.		
I use data to drive decision making and to adjust the learning.		
I understand and use instructional grouping to promote standards-based learning.		
I understand and use the components of standards-based unit and lesson design.		
I understand how to determine a student's prior knowledge.		
CLASSROOM ENVIRONMENT	YES	NO
I create and maintain a positive atmosphere of learning.		
I keep the focus on student learning.		
I use the appropriate teaching style to meet the needs of the lesson.		
I use a variety of teaching strategies that take into account the student's learning style.		
I check for understanding frequently.		
I provide for timely and meaningful feedback.		
I provide connections to past, present, and future learning.		
I manage time effectively.		
I frame the learning so that students know what is expected, how it will be assessed, and how it fits into real-world applications.		
I maximize the use of classroom space.		
I provide closure to the lessons.		
CLASSROOM MANAGEMENT	YES	NO
I actively monitor student learning.		
I analyze potential problem situations before they occur and explore various solutions.		
I am equitable and fair in handing down decisions.		
I provide consistent decisions on problem issues in conformance with the student handbook.		
I provide students with opportunities to learn and to use social behavior skills.		

The student is accountable for having the attitude of a learner: being willing to listen, being open to understanding new ideas, being willing to problem solve, having self-confidence to try new approaches, being able to adjust and revise, and wanting to communicate.

A truly unusual phenomenon that occurs throughout the educational system sometimes disrupts this accountability. Perhaps it's only paralleling the physical growth of the child or, maybe, there are other reasons relating to the social structure within families. It could all be hormonal; nevertheless, it all too often exists. In kindergarten and first grade, children are slightly leery of committing themselves totally to a teacher. The influence of the mother figure is so strong that the teacher works hard to win the students over. In fact, the phrase "But my mother said . . ." is the one these teachers often hear as a rebuttal of their own attempts to introduce new knowledge or social behaviors. In Grades 2 through 5, the teacher becomes a minor deity in the children's lives. Now, the phrase shifts from school to the home, and parents hear "But my teacher said . . ." as a sort of rebuttal to attempts to reinforce knowledge or social skills. The teacher is right in the students' minds. Grades 6 through 8 start to raise conflict in that students begin to play teachers and parents off each other, depending on whom the students need to support their own points. There is still an acceptance of both teacher and parent positions, but the student is not above questioning either or both. And following through on suggestions from either side is slow, at best. Grades 9 through 12 (with the exception of the last month of Grade 12 before graduation) are generally adversarial, with students questioning everything a teacher does or says. The students' value and judgment system is now considered to be superior to that of the teacher. Likewise, communication between student and parent is restricted to monosyllabic grunts of approval or disapproval. Only in the month before graduation is there an epiphany where the students, in all their wisdom, credit teachers and parents for their success. This tribute usually comes gushing out in graduation speeches as scholarships and awards are handed out.

What causes this shift from trust to mistrust is a study for behavioral specialists, but the consequences often create an accountability syndrome within the students that is counterproductive to their success. Therefore, students have to trust and respect their teacher; and they get this by seeing a teacher who is accountable to them as learners. When students see that someone is genuinely concerned about their success, that they are told up front what the performance objectives and assessments will be, that their ideas are valued and given a forum for expression and growth, that they have opportunities to practice their skills in real-world situations, that they can receive timely feedback so that they can modify and adjust their product, and that their continued progress toward a goal is more important than a single quiz, then they become active learners rather than just bodies filling up space.

Next on the accountability chain are the parents. Because they are in direct daily contact with the primary stakeholders, the students, their role cannot be underestimated. Their impact is what keeps the educational system moving. Not only are they financially accountable to the other taxpayers by keeping their children focused on the learning tasks so as not to waste resources, they are also responsible for providing opportunity and modeling for the students. Their accountability is summed up by the following conditions that have to be created and that should exist in the home.

- Guidelines and clear expectations of good behavior and positive academic performance

- Physical environment with space, facilities, and supplies for the student to do quality work at home

- Active support for student's needs and concerns

- Daily positive communication between the parent and student involving that day's work

- Active communication between the parent and the teacher on each other's needs and concerns involving the student

- Creation of a positive self-image within the student by modeling proper behavior, good grooming, appropriate dress, healthy lifestyle, and an affirmative attitude toward school and learning

- Acceptance of error, and emphasis on adjusting and revising

All of these responsibilities can best be summed up in the checklist in Figure 3.2. YES answers indicate parents who are actively involved in the student's education and who understand their responsibility to the accountability system. A NO answer shows where parents need to become more involved with the student, as well as with the school, in order to promote learning in the home. Guidance departments or administrative offices can provide information on how to overcome these negatives.

Figure 3.2   Parent Accountability Checklist

ACCOUNTABILITY	YES	NO
I set guidelines so my child can clearly understand the behaviors expected in the social world.		
I provide a clear understanding of what constitutes positive academic performance.		
I set clear objectives, as well as provide models, exemplars, and other assessment strategies available, so my child can self-monitor progress and growth.		
I communicate with my child daily, discussing accomplishments, needs, and problems.		
I communicate with the teacher to see how I can support the learning going on in the classroom.		
I help to design real-world learning application projects at home.		
I provide a place where my child can work with minimum disturbance, and that contains the necessary materials and supplies.		

WHAT MOST PEOPLE NEED TO KNOW

Middle managers are also important components in the accountability pyramid. Their duties put them closer to teachers and students on a daily basis, so they have a better opportunity and more time to gather data and to assist teachers in wise decision-making courses of action. Likewise, they can act as interim observers (designates of the principal) to correct unproductive teaching behaviors and to model positive ones. They function as confirmation agents to ensure that teachers and students are actively engaged in standards-based practices, and that administrators are providing the necessary feedback for teachers to make individual as well as grade-level adjustments. Their accountability is to do the following:

- Conduct weekly walkthroughs to make sure that standards-based teaching is going on in the classrooms (see Figure 3.3).
- Provide feedback on both productive and unproductive behaviors.
- Develop strategies to deal with underperforming teachers and students.
- Gather data for district interpretation.
- Motivate teachers to motivate students.
- Ensure that lines of communication are open with stakeholders.

WHAT SOME PEOPLE NEED TO KNOW

Although the student and teacher are the primary agents who interact within the classroom, other people also play critical roles. The administrator is a key figure in the accountability series primarily to do the following:

- Reinforce that standards-based education is going on in every classroom, all the time, for all the students.
- Observe teachers frequently and provide timely feedback.
- Provide training and professional development as needed.
- Advocate for and secure budgetary items necessary to ensure that teachers have access to materials, texts, and electronic resources.
- Provide a clearinghouse for data collection, assimilation, coordination, analysis, and distribution.
- Allow time to interact with teachers, parents, and students in an educational and nondisciplinary manner.

Although state departments of education set time-on-learning restrictions and dictate the minimum time necessary to constitute a school year, school administrators need to address and create or provide time within the framework of the school day to address issues involving observation (peer and administrative), feedback, training, and data collection. Time, or the lack of it, is no longer acceptable as an excuse for below average performance in a school or district. It should not be an excuse for average performance.

- The principal is actually the "lead teacher" and should model standards-based teaching practices.
- The principal has to provide meaningful feedback to the teachers to ensure accountability.
- Both the principal and the teacher must have a common document that outlines those elements that should exist in a standards-based lesson and classroom.
- The principal has to establish an ongoing dialogue with teachers before and after an observation has been made (see Figures 3.3 and 3.4).

Most school systems have forms in place that define the procedures and, often, the questions that will be asked before and after formal, contractually required observations. However, after brief walkthroughs (informal observations) or other longer visitations, the administrator must, likewise, have a conversation with the teacher to discuss the lesson being observed. This dialogue should be conducted in a nonthreatening manner so the teacher self-examines the lesson and reflects on ways to adjust and revise.

Figure 3.3 Walkthrough Guide

TEACHER	DATE	TIME	OBSERVATION	SUGGESTION

Limit the observation and suggestion to one specific thing. If major problems are witnessed, schedule a meeting with the teacher immediately to discuss ways to change. In either regard, the administrator should have a dialogue with the teacher about the observation. The Walkthrough Dialogue Guide in Figure 3.4 lists seven questions that will help to promote the discussion. The sooner after the original walkthrough observation that this dialogue can be conducted, the better. The teacher's recollection and introspection are what drive the need for improvement and the overall growth of instruction.

Teachers should take the time to do a self-examination (see Figure 3.5) in order to scrutinize what they have done in the classroom in relationship to what they wanted to do. This self-inquiry allows the teacher to reflect back and make adjustments to the teaching that has an immediate impact for the students' learning.

The administrator is encouraged to follow through on any issues lingering after a walkthrough.

- Rule 1: Keeping students busy is not a teacher's primary function; keeping students learning is.
- Rule 2: If no one sees learning taking place, then it probably isn't taking place.
- Rule 3: Check for understanding; don't assume anything.

Figure 3.4 Walkthrough Dialogue

SAMPLE QUESTIONS
1. How do you think the lesson went today?
2. What do you think the students got out of the lesson?
3. If you were to do the lesson over, is there anything you would change? Why?
4. What will you do to tie this lesson into tomorrow's learning?
5. What problems do you foresee?
6. What are some strategies that you will use to overcome these potential problems?
7. Is there any way that I can help?

Figure 3.5   Teacher Lesson Self-Examination

Lesson Subject: _____ Time: _____

How do you think the lesson went today?	Excellent	Good	Average	Poor
What is your basis for making this decision? Be specific.				
What do you think the students got out of the lesson?				
What did you want them to get out of the lesson?				
If you were to do the lesson over, is there anything you would change? Why?				
What will you do to tie this lesson in to tomorrow's learning?				
What problems, if any, do you foresee?				
What strategies will you use to overcome these potential problems?				

Most school systems already have formal observation forms that entail more of a summative (final evaluation) than a walkthrough type (formative or ongoing aid to allow correction and adjustment). The rubric in Figure 3.6 may be used to address longer classroom observations.

The observation rubric can then be used as the basis of feedback for the teacher. Areas of strength can be listed and a narrative can be provided to reinforce them. Likewise, general suggestions can be written to assist the teacher in improving specific areas.

Major elements of immediate concern (those with designations of 2 and 1) can be immediately addressed through mentoring, teacher assistance programs, professional development, use of paraprofessionals, or peer teams. The form, as well as the teacher's lesson plans and assessments, is a method of data collection concerning teacher accountability. Praising a teacher's strengths is just as important as citing weaknesses. Unless the violations of classroom procedure are so excessive as to require the immediate removal of the teacher from the environment, the dialogue should focus on positive steps of improvement.

Part two of the form (see Figure 3.7) would be used at a meeting between the teacher and the administrator in which the teacher would have filled out the form providing the performance objectives that were the goal, the strategies that were used, and the data obtained through student performance assessments that showed to what degree the objective had been met.

The administrator has both the duty and the obligation to create a standards-based environment predicated on the belief that all students can and should learn. In addition, the accountability lies in nourishing a community of student-centered education where the measurement of success is student achievement.

SUMMARY

Educational accountability involves being answerable, responsible, and liable for the learning taking place. Each person in the accountability pyramid, the administrator, teacher, student, and parent, is answerable and responsible to ensure that standards-based education is being emphasized and used throughout the school district.

- The teacher's role is to create an educational environment that focuses on student learning and uses data to make critical decisions.
- The student's role is to utilize the educational resources to grow as a scholar and as an individual.
- The parent's role is to provide support by creating opportunities for the student to apply the learning.
- The administrator's role is to keep all of the stakeholders focused on the mission at hand: student growth.

Figure 3.6   Observation Rubric

TEACHER:	GRADE:
OBSERVER:	DATE:

Level of Performance: 4 = Advanced; 3 = Proficient; 2 = Average; 1 = Needs Improvement

ELEMENTS OF STANDARDS-BASED INSTRUCTION	4	3	2	1
The standards are displayed openly and clearly in the classroom.				
The standards are written in a grade-appropriate language.				
The teacher has explained the importance of learning the standards and their relevance to in-class and real-world application.				
The teacher has provided a clear, observable, and measurable objective to the class.				
The teacher has checked to see that the students understand the requirements of the objective.				
The students have helped to create or were given a method to assess their work (rubric, exemplar, model, etc.).				
The teacher has gone over the lesson components so students understand what the end product should be.				
The teacher has provided students with the opportunity to connect the lesson to previous learning.				
The teacher has demonstrated a high level of content knowledge.				
The teacher has employed a variety of strategies to motivate student learning.				
The teacher has used a variety of strategies to check for understanding frequently, and to adjust instruction accordingly.				
The teacher has made sure the use of time and space are appropriate to the lesson.				
The teacher has provided lesson differentiation as necessary.				
The teacher has provided scaffolding and support as necessary.				
The teacher has provided students with the opportunity to apply and practice the learning and skills in authentic situations.				
The teacher has allowed students the opportunity to use multiple methods of presentation.				
The teacher has tied the learning in to other disciplines.				
The teacher has provided incentives for students to exceed the expectations.				
The teacher has maintained a positive learning environment.				
The teacher has designed closure to the lesson.				
COMMENTS				
GENERAL SUGGESTIONS				
IMMEDIATE CONCERNS				

Figure 3.7 Observation Follow-Up

TEACHER: DATE:

PERFORMANCE OBJECTIVE	STRATEGY	DATA THAT SUPPORTS SUCCESS
AREAS TEACHER REQUESTS ASSISTANCE		

Performance Objective 4

One of the characters in the old Doc Savage pulp paperback series loved to use a highly charged extensive vocabulary to explain very simple actions. His colleagues always questioned what he was saying and constantly asked, "Why can't you just tell us what you want us to do?" The term *performance objective* is actually the answer to that question; it's what a teacher wants students to be able to do to show they have learned the skills required and can use them. The two key words in that definition are *do* and *show*. Both of them require the student to perform something that is visible or audible to the observer.

Think about being in a theater and watching a magician, complete with cape, top hat, and wand, step forward onto the empty stage. The patter goes something like this: "Ladies and gentlemen, tonight, on this stage, I intend to produce a 60-pound rabbit from this hat that is now on my head." The magician takes off the hat, shows it to be empty inside and out, and then holds it at arm's length. Members of the audience immediately realize that the hat is incapable of holding a rabbit of that size. Similarly, audience members are not sure whether a rabbit of 60 pounds has ever existed. With the hat in his left hand and the wand in his right, the magician starts to chant out loud. At that moment, the lights go out leaving total blackness throughout the theater. The magician continues to chant for a few seconds then says, "Voilà! Ladies and gentlemen, Rosco, the 60-pound rabbit." The sound of taped applause fills the darkened theater. "Now, if my assistant would take Rosco away, we can continue." The sound of footsteps goes in one direction, stops, and then reverses direction. When they fade, the lights come back on, and the magician is standing in the center of the stage, putting the hat back on his head and saying, "Now, for my second trick, I'd like to saw a woman in half."

Theoretically, the magician has done something, but the action has not been observed. The members of the audience don't know if a 60-pound rabbit was really produced from the hat or if a rabbit that size even exists. After the clamor of "We were cheated!" dies down, the next demand is "Do it again! Only this time with the lights on." Saying or thinking that someone can do something is not the same as seeing it being done and judging how successfully it was performed. Therefore, a performance objective requires someone to do the following:

- Clearly show a skill has been learned and mastered.
- Be able to use that skill in ongoing demonstrations to prove that the first time wasn't an accident.

TOUCHING ALL THE BASES BUT GETTING THROWN OUT AT HOME

An administrator was observing a teacher. Making sure that the teaching exhibition would cover all of the required bases, the educator spent a great deal of time preparing activities for the class. Supplies were readied; work sheets were run off; and overheads were arranged for presentation. Every minute of the class time would be occupied by a quiz, a review of act three of the play they were studying, and the project the teacher had assigned. Numerous handouts were circulated: one was the grammar quiz, another had questions about the play, and the last contained measurement charts of parts of the project. There were no behavior incidents throughout the entire period. At the end of the class, the students handed in the scissors and colored pencils as well as the work sheets, gathered their books, and exited for their next subject. The administrator approached the smiling teacher and asked, "What did you want the students to learn today?" The teacher responded by citing a list of skills that the students were supposed to exhibit. The administrator then asked if the teacher had told the students what they were supposed to learn. Sheepishly, the teacher's smile turned to a look of discomfort. "No . . . not really" was the weak response. The administrator then asked how the teacher was going to know that what they learned was what the teacher expected. Lastly, the observer said that while the lesson looked nice, what did it have to do with the standards that were supposed to be covered? A list of activities is not a performance objective in much the same way that a menu is not a meal.

One of the dangers of teaching is forgetting that the classroom is driven by student learning and not just by teacher teaching. Performance objectives are critical in keeping both students and teachers focused on the bottom line: learning. For students, a performance objective explains what they are expected to know and be able to do, as well as what skills and knowledge they are expected to learn. For teachers, performance objectives pinpoint what skills and knowledge will be taught, what instructional methods will be used to teach them, and what assessments will prove that they have been learned. The whole scenario hinges not on what a teacher plans to do but on what students will be able to do.

WHAT EVERYONE NEEDS TO KNOW

Performance objectives provide the focal point for a lesson in that they bring all of the components and strategies together to address the primary question:

What do you want students to know and be able to do? In that regard, everyone needs to know that a performance objective meets all the following criteria:

- Be written in specific language so that the learner has no question about what is expected

- Be measurable so someone can see to what extent the material has been learned and can be used

- Be observable so someone can see or hear it being used correctly and frequently

- Relate to the standard; it must be relevant and not just relative

- Be consistent with the learning, drawing a connection with what has been learned and linking it to what comes next

- Be achievable and masterable

- Be manageable given restrictions of time

- Should have tie to the real world

Figure 4.1 outlines and defines the three components of a performance objective and gives examples to demonstrate how a performance objective might be created.

The primary focus for the performance objective is to provide a way for the students to gain and apply the learning in a manner that measures their success and informs the instructor that the standard has been mastered. Figure 4.2 contains a few tips that the teacher should keep in mind when creating performance objectives.

Figure 4.1   Performance Objectives

PARTS	DEFINITION	EXAMPLES
Conditions	Describes the circumstances under which the task must be performed (when, where, limits, restrictions, and so on).	Using a grid, . . . Using only five paragraphs, . . . Using a skeletal chart, . . .
Task	This is the action the learner must perform (it must be stated as an action verb), which is measurable and observable. Begin each task with: "You (the student) will be able to . . ."	. . . you will be able to draw an arc connecting point A to point B . . . . . . you will be able to write a persuasive essay . . . . . . you will be able to identify three types of teeth in the human head . . .
Criteria	This is the measurable part that the learners must meet to determine if they are successful.	. . . passing through at least three grid quadrants. . . . citing three governmental sources on the dangers of global warming. . . . by drawing them and listing their functions.

Figure 4.2   Performance Objective Tips

♦ Avoid verbs open to interpretation, such as *believe, grasp, understand, think,* and *feel.* Use terms that describe observable behaviors, such as *draw, name, list, describe,* and *calculate.*

♦ To see if the objective is measurable, try the "Look at me" test: "Look at me while I (state the task here)." If the person you are addressing can see it, the task is measurable. For example: "Look at me while I identify all the parts of a flower."

♦ Be clear about the expectations so that the students understand what is required:

  ○ Condition: While riding a unicycle, . . .
  ○ Task: . . . you will juggle three balls . . .
  ○ Criteria: . . . for 30 seconds.

♦ Write the criteria in the form of a rubric:

TASK	4	3	2	1
Dexterity	Juggling three balls for 30 seconds	Juggling three balls for 20 seconds	Juggling three balls for 10 seconds	Juggling three balls for less than 10 seconds
Balance	Riding the unicycle for 30 seconds	Riding the unicycle for 20 seconds	Riding the unicycle for 10 seconds	Riding the unicycle for less than 10 seconds

• Create a scale. For example: Points: 8 = Advanced (Mastered, Exemplary), 7 = Proficient, 6 = At Grade Level, 5 or Lower = Beginning (Below Grade Level).
• Make sure the students have a copy of the rubric and understand it completely.
• Make sure the objective is results-oriented. It must be attainable within the time allowed and the environment in which the performance must take place.
• Use the following verbs and others like them to demonstrate knowledge, application, and problem solving:

KNOWLEDGE	Compare, contrast, define, describe, identify, list, name, paraphrase, summarize, restate
APPLICATION	Calculate, draw, estimate, give example, locate, measure, factor, map, perform, solve, write, use, outline
PROBLEM SOLVING	Assess, choose, construct, create, criticize, debate, judge, design, organize, recommend

♦ Make sure the performance objective is reality based and relevant. It must be relevant not only to in-class application but also to the world outside of the classroom in order to have meaning for the students.

♦ The teacher must help the students tie in the previous learning to the present learning in the performance objective in order to have students make critical connections.

♦ Make sure the performance objective relates directly to the standard(s) that the students are learning.

♦ The focus has to be centered on what the student has to do to demonstrate what has been learned rather than on what the instructor has taught.

   ○ *Poor objective:* The teacher will explain how the use of introductory adverbial clauses can vary sentence beginnings.

   ○ *Better objective:* The student will vary a sentence beginning by using an introductory adverbial clause.

♦ The performance objective must deal with what can reasonably be expected from a student after the instruction and practice are provided. The objective should not be too general or too specific.

   ○ *Poor objectives:*

     ■ The student will create a series of laboratory experiments to test for elements contained in air. (too general)

     ■ The student will name a noun that begins with the letter Z. (too specific)

     ■ The student will identify the formula for finding the circumference of a circle. (too specific)

   ○ *Better Objectives:*

     ■ The student will conduct a laboratory experiment to determine how much oxygen a one-foot-high tomato plant gives off in an hour.

     ■ The student will underline all of the nouns once and the proper nouns twice in Lincoln's Gettysburg Address.

     ■ The student will use the formula for finding the circumference of a circle to determine how large of a circular swimming pool will fit into a rectangular backyard with one side being 24 feet and the other being 50 feet.

The templates in Figures 4.3, 4.4, and 4.5 deal with performance objectives involving standards that can be applied to mathematics, science, and English language arts. They are intended to provide a working format for teachers to create performance objectives that meet all of the requirements of emphasizing what students are supposed to know and be able to do successfully. They cover all of the areas of condition, task, and criteria. Assessment pieces are covered in a later chapter.

Figure 4.3   Sample Performance Objective #1

Class: Period A 6th Grade English Language Arts   **Date:**

Standard(s): Students will demonstrate an understanding that many words in Standard American English are borrowed from other languages.

Conditions: Using a table with three columns (one marked COMMONLY USED WORDS, another marked ORIGINS, and a third marked DEFINITIONS) . . .

Task: . . . the student will be able to list, identify, and define all of the Greek and Latin words . . .

Criteria: . . . found in the first four amendments to the Constitution of the United States of America.

Figure 4.4   Sample Performance Objective #2

Class: Period B 4th Grade Science	**Date:**

Standard(s): Students will display an understanding of the properties of objects and materials, such as the similarities and differences in size and weight.

Conditions: Using a square box (6″ high, 6″ wide, 6″ deep) . . .

Task: . . . the student will completely fill and weigh the box four different times: first empty; second with fine grain sand; third with granulated sugar; and fourth with processed flour . . .

Criteria: . . . then list the differences in weights among the three substances and draw two conclusions and explanations about why the weights differ.

Figure 4.5   Sample Performance Objective #3

Class: Period A 8th Grade Mathematics	**Date:**

Standard(s): Students will demonstrate an understanding of how to solve for the unknown or undecided quantities using algebra, graphing, sound reasoning, and other strategies.

Conditions: Using X as the unknown and a sold-out stadium of 15,000 seats . . .

Task: . . . the student will calculate exactly how many child-sized baseball caps must be ordered if they are to be given free to each child accompanied by a parent (each parent or both parents bring only one child) . . .

Criteria: . . . if one-third of the children are accompanied by a single parent and the remainder are accompanied by both parents.

The checklist in Figure 4.6 defines what the teacher should do.

Parents should ask teachers to see performance objectives so they know how those objectives compare with the standards and how they are assessed. Likewise, in helping their children to practice at home, parents can use the teacher practice sheet to design their own performance objectives with the students, and assist them to practice and apply their learning.

Figure 4.6   Teacher Checklist

PERFORMANCE OBJECTIVE	YES	NO
Used verbs that described observable behaviors.		
Checked to see if the objective was measurable.		
Was clear about the expectations so that the students understood what was required.		
Often wrote the criteria in the form of a rubric.		
Made sure the students had a copy of the rubric and understood it.		
Made sure the objective was attainable within the time allowed and the environment in which the performance took place.		
Made sure the performance objective was reality based and relevant.		
Tied in the previous learning to the present learning.		
Made sure the performance objective related directly to the standard(s) that the students were learning.		
Made sure the focus was centered on what the student had to do to demonstrate what had been learned rather than on what the instructor had taught.		

WHAT MOST PEOPLE NEED TO KNOW

All too often, people are hired to do one job but are then asked, cajoled, or ordered to take on extra responsibilities that interfere with the positional duties they were originally asked to assume. Keeping that in mind, school systems need to focus on the fact that teachers were hired to teach; all of their actions should be directed toward that capacity rather than toward secretarial and policing positions.

- Teachers need time to create meaningful performance objectives. Keeping class size small, if possible, contributes greatly to giving teachers the time to design effective performance objectives and to differentiate them. The old "if you can teach one student, you can teach 40 students" has been proven to be false in its assumption that each student will learn at the same pace.

- A teacher's place is in the classroom; bus duties, cafeteria monitoring, hall policing, and study hall surveillance should be mainly structured to aides and paraprofessionals, or hired monitors, to free up teacher time for educational interaction with students and peer conferencing.

WHAT SOME PEOPLE NEED TO KNOW

First, teachers need the opportunity to hone their craft through support systems and professional development. One of the most widespread, mistaken notions in education is that if you give teachers all of the information, they can turn around and use it immediately. True teachers are, foremost, learners; as such, they need practice, data, and assessments to adjust their performance. Second, educators need support—moral and financial—as well as feedback.

- Teachers need professional development and practice to become adept at writing performance objectives that contain all of the required parts, are relevant, and are standards based.

- Budgets must be in place and organizational design must be structured to relieve teachers of secretarial and monitoring duties and to keep them focused on providing exemplary standards-based instruction.

- Administration, school committees, and unions must realize that time and training are key components in creating a strong and effective educational community. Collaborative thinking is often necessary to secure that time by thinking outside the box.

SUMMARY

Performance objectives are critical pieces in the chain of standards-based education. They provide the focus for student learning and the goal for student assessment. Likewise, they are the crucial components in answering the basic educational question: What is a student supposed to know and be able to do?

- Performance objectives are necessary to provide direction for both students and teachers.

- Performance objectives are made up of three parts: condition, task, and criteria.

- Performance objectives must address the learning that is taking place, the time available, and the environment in which the objective will occur.

- The performance objective must be learner centered.

- The performance objective must be measurable, relate to the standard being covered, have a real-world tie, and be reachable.

Performance Assessment 5

I n George Orwell's *1984*, the real terror is not that the protagonist, Winston Smith, is destroyed, because few of the readers actually identify with him. Instead, the uneasy gnawing in most people's stomachs is how easily all of this world conquest has been done. When O'Brien, Big Brother's spokesman, says that the future is a boot smashing a human face, forever (Orwell, 1949, p. 220) and that the ideal future language will be "doubleplus duckspeak," a series of incomprehensible quacks (p. 254), the mind of the reader races to find a way to beat the Party. But first, the logical person must figure out what the bottom line is. In other words, one must decide what basic steps the Party has taken to begin and eventually maintain total control. The answer then becomes obvious—eliminate all standards of comparison. The reason for this is that as long as a person has a standard against which to weigh hope, behavior, comfort, communication, and everything else that makes us human, there will be progress and growth. But once the standard is eliminated, stagnation and regression become inevitable. Even with a standard in place, growth is sometimes stifled because the standard is too far removed from the reality of our experiences. Therefore, to achieve advancement, a standard must exist, and it must be based upon real-world application. At that point, only one thing is missing; people must have assessments in order to know how well they are doing in mastering and applying the standard. In the novel, the standards were removed and the people stopped progressing. But it's a work of fiction. In the real world, standards exist. Your car is built and rated upon performance standards; your medicine is made according to high standards of quality; even this book is printed according to standards. If one of these standards is compromised, a recall is issued. When a plane crashes, standards of design, operation, and service are all scrutinized to find the reason for the accident. Agencies check to see which standard has been violated, and recommendations are made to increase compliance or to redesign the end product. In short, standards are the key by which society operates.

Not surprisingly, this whole book is about standards. It's about standards for students, parents, teachers, schools, and districts. In addition, since every school district in the country is operating on some type of educational standards, this text serves to integrate state standards with federal standards. But that being said, how does anyone know if the standards are being met or, for that matter, to what degree they're being met? How do students know when they are succeeding and when they should be making adjustments? How do teachers know when students have mastered a standard and can move on to new learning or when additional review or even reteaching is necessary? How do teachers know when a student can apply knowledge in different learning environments successfully (such as using writing skills to explain a math solution)? How do parents know when students are being challenged or just being confused? The answers to all of these questions have to do with performance assessments.

WHAT? WHERE? WHY? HOW?

Typically, four main questions relate to performance assessments:

- What are they?
- Where did they come from? Are they new or have they always been around?
- Why are they so important? Do they have a specific purpose?
- How are they used?

To answer these questions, the reader has to get a brief review of the history of assessments. In the past, the emphasis of assessments was on the following:

- Assessing what was easily measured
- Assessing the knowledge level in Bloom's Taxonomy
- Assessing to find out what students didn't know
- Generally using end-of-unit testing as evidence of a grade

In the present, the emphasis has shifted away from the old criteria and toward the following:

- Assessing what skills are highly valued
- Assessing understanding, reasoning, and application
- Assessing to learn what students do know
- Teaching students how to self-assess in order to correct and adjust

So now that we know a little about the past and present of assessments, let's take a look at how all of this connects with the four basic questions: What? Where? Why? How?

Performance assessments are tools that allow students to see how they are doing on a predetermined scale of success. In addition, many performance assessments provide specific areas that students can examine to see what they need to concentrate on in order to improve the quality of their understanding and application skills. Assessments let people know how they can improve. In this way, students can better focus on what is important to know, rather than on what is nice to know, and they can see and build upon their strengths. Therefore, students are empowered rather than enabled.

A second benefit of assessments is that they provide important data to teachers so they can make critical adjustments to their presentation methods and strategies when they can have the most impact. Likewise, assessments give teachers and students a common vocabulary with which to communicate their needs to each other, as well as to parents.

Finally, by using the data provided by the assessments, administrators can make more informed important decisions involving budgetary considerations, allocation of resources, teacher training, professional development, strategic use of time, and communication with and through the educational community.

SUMMATIVE AND FORMATIVE

All assessments usually fall into two categories: *summative* and *formative*. The way to determine which category a particular assessment falls under is by examining the differences between the two types.

Summative assessments are generally exams or tests given at the end of a unit of learning. They are often fill-in, multiple choice, true or false, or essay question in origin. The following are generally ways that teachers use these assessments:

- To pass or fail a student after a unit, semester, or year (such as A–F or 100–60)

- To rank a student in relation to peers (65th out of 300 seniors)

- To show that a student can progress to a higher level of study in a sequential course (Spanish I to Spanish II, and so on)

- To assure suitability for a skill program (such as driver's license test, master plumber license test, law exam, or Realtor's license exam)

- To predict success in future work or to select a field of study (such as aptitude test, police academy exam)

- To signal suitability for educational advancement, employment, or promotion (college entrance exam, SAT, or police captain's test)

- To provide a source of data that allows the teacher to judge the effectiveness of the instruction in order to make changes at a future time (such as 65% passed the test)

Summative assessments are usually given after a unit of study has been completed so that the data these tests produce usually doesn't have an immediate impact on a student's performance during the designated learning. For example, because the results of final exams come too late to help the student correct and adjust, their main use is to help a teacher revise the curriculum, delivery strategies, or assessments for the future.

In comparison, formative assessments are those that are used by the teacher for the following:

- To provide feedback to students so they can adjust and correct while doing the project or lesson
- To provide motivation for students by allowing them to focus on specific areas of concern while acknowledging areas of exemplary performance
- To evaluate a student's strengths and weaknesses
- To provide rubrics, models, or exemplars to assist the student in developing a sense of responsibility for the learning
- To provide a source of immediate and ongoing data to assist teachers to make sound educational decisions impacting the present learners

The data from formative assessments is used both by the teacher and the student to make ongoing adjustments to the learning that is taking place at that moment.

Summative assessments tell students how they did, while formative assessments tell them how they are doing. Summative assessments look more at a group's performance, usually one time, using the data so the instructor can evaluate both the materials and the learning process for future revision. Formative assessments are focused more at the individual performance, multiple times, with the intention to improve that performance as soon as possible.

ELIMINATE A AND D; GUESS B OR C

While summative assessments have their place, many of them are susceptible to educated guessing. In other words, students have found ways to interpret and beat the tests without really applying the knowledge that the test is supposed to measure. The game then becomes one of analyzing the structure and rationale behind the test and applying rules of psychology and common sense. Unfortunately, although these may be valuable thinking skills, they are not being used for the intended purpose, which is to demonstrate the focus of the learning being tested.

And this happens on all levels. For example, untold numbers of books are available that teach readers how to beat the SATs. These manuals explain how to employ strategies to narrow down the guesswork into a manageable level of risk, how to analyze the mind-set of the test makers, and how to arrive at the number of points a person needs to manipulate in each of the test categories. They also show that you can skip a certain number of questions or answer all of the questions in one specific category. Similarly, students in true-false tests use this same analysis. They start with the assumption that the answers aren't all true or all false. Once this is established, students then look for patterns to emerge and base their decisions on how the answer sheet starts to look rather than on what the questions ask. As a result, many summative tests don't really demonstrate the depth of understanding a student may have or may need in order to advance.

Furthermore, summative assessments are usually given in a short, fixed period, so they don't take into consideration that a student's pet died that morning, a skirt ripped, an illness struck the night before, a friendship broke up, a major pimple appeared, or countless other problems that affected the emotional state of the test taker at the moment when clarity of thought was required.

Because of the limitations of summative assessments, this chapter focuses on formative assessments, specifically those dealing with performance objectives that are used when the learning is taking place. It also touches on some of the ideas that Eric Jensen promotes in his book, *Teaching With the Brain in Mind* (1998), such as the fact that conditions that tend to eliminate the motivation to learn are threat, intimidation, negative competition (pitting one student against another), and infrequent or unclear feedback. Those things that increase motivation are providing a sense of choice, increasing the frequency and the specificity of feedback, raising the level of concern without raising the fear or threat level, and using self-assessment. Because formative assessments emphasize choice, feedback, and self-assessment, the focus here is on showing how these elements can help students to adjust their level of performance and enhance the quality of their learning.

WHAT EVERYONE NEEDS TO KNOW

One of the most important aspects of formative assessments is that they provide almost immediate and ongoing feedback, so both teachers and students have the necessary short-term data to alter and adjust performance. Since the emphasis is on learning and applying rather than on simply testing, students are often more willing to be active participants in the process.

- Performance objectives are often composed of open-ended, multistep problem-solving situations that require feedback in the form of formative assessments.

- Performance objectives require students to use prior knowledge and present learning to create solutions and to demonstrate the results in an observable manner. Formative assessments give students this opportunity more often.

- Formative assessments can assist the teacher in seeing how the student will demonstrate the use of the skills in the classroom, and in real-world applications.

The teacher can use any of a number of strategies to assess student learning and to provide immediate feedback. Similarly, most of these same strategies can also be used by the students to self-assess. In this way, students keep building on their strengths while concentrating on ways to eliminate their areas of concern. They quickly understand that they have more than one opportunity to get something right without being penalized. Learning becomes more of a process than a series of events that may appear in isolation from each other.

ASSESSMENT STRATEGIES

Teachers can use a variety of formative assessment strategies; often more than one can be used at the same time (observation and checklist or rubric).

Observation: This is a direct method for seeing what students can and cannot do, either working individually or in groups. In this way, the teacher may focus on the following:

- How the students use resources
- How they use social interaction skills, and how they process and apply learning
- How they make necessary connections
- How they use organizational skills

Typically, the observation begins after the students are informed of the standard upon which they will be working, the objective of the lesson, the performance requirements that will demonstrate what they have learned and how they can apply it, and the criteria that demonstrate success.

The teacher can use note cards or self-sticking note sheets to record data about students for use in planning lessons. Some of these cards can be given to students as the teacher walks around. The process doesn't disturb the class, gives quick feedback, and provides ideas as to how the student can correct and adjust.

Figure 5.1   Note Cards for Planning Lessons

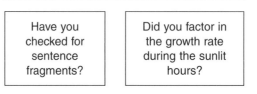

| Have you checked for sentence fragments? | Did you factor in the growth rate during the sunlit hours? |

Exemplars: These are pieces of student work that have been collected because they demonstrate levels of accomplishment in regard to the standard or skill on which the students are presently working. The exemplars usually show degrees of success ranging from *Unfinished* through *At Grade Level* all the way to *Advanced.* Students are able to see those elements in their own work, compare them to the exemplar levels, and correct, adjust, and revise. Therefore, the students are using a standard of comparison.

However, for this to work, the teacher has to obtain these exemplars from whatever sources are available. Some of these can be culled from previous classes; other samples might exist in state department of education resource banks; still others are available in online Web sites. Exemplars are a powerful assessment tool since they allow students the opportunity to see what their product should resemble. When using exemplars, the teacher must be sure that each one clearly identifies what elements within it constitute quality work. An essay, math solution, or science experiment is useless as an exemplar unless the specific qualities that make it significant are pointed out. Students should have a range of exemplars so they know on what step of development they presently are. Practice in using exemplars is important since students must be taught what to look for and how to adjust or correct it in their own product.

Models: All preconstructed or purchased representations that provide a sensory experience for the student by physically defining what the outcome of the performance objective should resemble are known as models. For example, if the students were to create a depiction of Atlas holding the world on his shoulders, a globe might serve to help students identify the relative size of the continents. Whether the students were making a clay representation or drawing a picture, the relative size of the water and land masses would be close to reality. The globe would assist students in estimating the dimensions. Likewise, a model of the Wright Brothers' plane serves as a visual guide in helping students to estimate the size of the wingspan necessary to provide lift. The model itself acts as a rubric, a guide through the process, as well as a standard of comparison on the end product.

Another example involved a teacher who showed students a drawing of Shakespeare's stage and asked them to re-create it to better understand the physical dimensions and constraints under which the playwright operated. Two boys in the class, one of whom was the son of a doctor, used tongue depressors glued together to represent the stage. They gathered the measurements and re-created the stage to scale, always going back to the model to check for accuracy.

Narrative: A narrative is a short piece written about an aspect of a student's performance. Think of it as another column in a rubric that specifically clarifies the criteria and levels of performance by identifying areas of strength and weakness. Recently, an admissions officer said that colleges don't rely as much on the results of entrance exams as they once did. The individual stated that the letters of recommendation sent on the student's behalf are higher on the list. These narratives sum up the student's educational performance and ability, personality, social awareness, and potential for the future. Like these longer counterparts, assessment narratives give immediate feedback to the students (see Figure 5.2).

Checklist: A list of statements or points that the student or teacher needs to understand or accomplish in relationship to a performance objective is known as a checklist. The student or teacher can respond by checking off YES or NO. The checklist is a quick way to self-assess the relationship to the final goal (see Figures 5.3 and 5.4).

Rubrics: Scoring guides with required criteria and degrees of success noted are called rubrics. They define quality in the work and help students and teachers to determine where a student is on the road to mastery. Rubrics help to make teacher descriptions clearer since they provide descriptors of the criteria necessary to reach levels of success. They may also list specific areas for students to address to ensure the quality and applicability of the final product. Students can judge their own work, making corrections and revisions, thereby reducing the teacher time that's often spent in numerous and extensive evaluations. Rubrics provide more immediate feedback necessary for revising the work in progress. Lastly, the rubrics provide teachers and students with a common language, which can be shared with parents, so that all of the stakeholders are

Figure 5.2   Sample Narrative

CRITERIA	LEVEL OF PERFORMANCE	NARRATIVE
RESPONDING TO QUESTIONS GROUP WORK	SLIGHTLY BELOW GRADE LEVEL	You rarely volunteer and must be called on. You don't ask any questions during class and often have difficulty understanding what is required in the problem-solving part of the lesson. In group work, you sit passively but do the work.
STUDENT RESPONSE:		
RESOLUTION:		

Figure 5.3   Sample Teacher Checklist

	YES	NO
I determined the students' prior knowledge.	_____	_____
I tied the lesson to the standards.	_____	_____
I made sure the performance objective was clear.	_____	_____
I involved the students in creating the rubric.	_____	_____
I accommodated different learning styles.	_____	_____
I provided differentiated lessons.	_____	_____
I provided appropriate scaffolding.	_____	_____
I provided clear and immediate feedback.	_____	_____
I provided students the opportunity to work in groups.	_____	_____

on the same page when communicating with each other. Teachers must remember that rubrics are not necessary if everyone in the class can already score at the highest levels.

The most frequent method for creating rubrics is by using a grid, because it's both easy to read as well as simple to understand. It lists the criteria (those aspects of the work that tie into the standard and the performance objective) in a downward column on the left and levels of performance (descriptors that tell

Figure 5.4 Sample Student Writing Checklist

	YES	NO
I checked for spelling.	____	____
I checked to see if I capitalized proper nouns.	____	____
I made sure I used a topic sentence in each paragraph.	____	____
I used transition words between sentences.	____	____
I use quotation marks for direct quotes.	____	____
I varied the beginnings of sentences.	____	____
I eliminated sentence fragments.	____	____
I was not redundant.	____	____
I made sure all pronouns had clear antecedents.	____	____
I checked subject-verb agreement.	____	____

Figure 5.5 Sample Rubric Format

CRITERIA LEVELS OF PERFORMANCE

	LEVEL 4 MASTERY	LEVEL 3 PROFICIENCY	LEVEL 2 AVERAGE	LEVEL 1 NEEDS WORK
Criteria 1	**Descriptor** "You have it and can apply it successfully every time."	**Descriptor** "You have it and can apply it successfully."	**Descriptor** "You have it but are having difficulty in . . . ."	**Descriptor** "You don't have it, yet."
Criteria 2	**Descriptor** "You have it and can apply it successfully every time."	**Descriptor** "You have it and can apply it successfully."	**Descriptor** "You have it but are having difficulty in . . . ."	**Descriptor** "You don't have it, yet."
Criteria 3	**Descriptor** "You have it, plus more, and can apply it successfully."	**Descriptor** "You have it and can apply it successfully."	**Descriptor** "You have it but are having difficulty in . . . ."	**Descriptor** "You don't have it, yet."
Criteria 4	**Descriptor** "You have it, plus more, and can apply it successfully."	**Descriptor** "You have it and can apply it successfully."	**Descriptor** "You have it but are having difficulty in . . . ."	**Descriptor** "You don't have it, yet."

the students where they are on the progression toward mastery) that read across to the right (see Figure 5.5). Teachers and students would be wise to restrict the number to four or five; after that, the process becomes too picky.

Other terms that may be used as descriptors for the performance levels include the following:

- Level 4: Exemplary, Exceeds Expectations, Superior, Advanced
- Level 3: Meets Expectations, Good, Above Grade Level
- Level 2: Progressing, At Grade Level, Fair
- Level 1: Not Yet There, Needs Improvement, Incomplete

In describing specific criteria, the following terms might be used to express range of achievement.

- *Accuracy:* Level 4, Precise (All Facts Documented); Level 3, Most Facts Documented; Level 2, Vague (Some Facts Documented); Level 1, Imprecise (Few Facts Documented)
- *Mechanics:* Level 4, No Errors; Level 3, Few Errors (Two or Less); Level 2, Some Errors (Five or Less); Level 1, Frequent Errors (More Than Five)
- *Vocabulary Usage:* Level 4, Rich, Varied; Level 3, Varied but Occasionally Repetitive; Level 2, Simple With Much Repetition; Level 1, Misused With Very Much Repetition
- *Content:* Level 4, Fully Developed; Level 3, Adequately Developed; Level 2, Partially Developed; Level 1, Undeveloped

Depending on the extent of the performance objective, rubrics might concentrate on more specifics that are important in the present learning. The following sample performance objective addresses an expository writing piece for a fifth grade English language arts class. The original short story traces the author's reflections on getting her puppy, Molly, a long time ago and now having to take her to be put down. The sample rubric that follows (see Figure 5.6) is intended to address topic development and oral presentation skills, as well as some of the English conventions being studied and reinforced.

By adhering to the preceding performance objective and rubric, the learner is able to assess ongoing progress, knowing specifically what is required for each level of growth. In conjunction, by circling the appropriate level of performance the student has attained for each criterion, the teacher provides quick and meaningful feedback for the learner. Students then can easily identify those skills and standards that need more work. Once the students have revised the pieces of work to their maximum potential, then the total points can be added and an appropriate status assigned. The teacher can move on to other standards and skills or use the status category and the rubric to deal with individual problems. In this way, both the teacher and the student can quickly see where the student has strengths and weaknesses. While this may seem time-consuming, teachers often devise strategies to pick up the necessary minutes: they may move around the classroom and speak to individual students as others are writing; create groups of students to foster discussion with peers; utilize time-out moments when students are given an opportunity to reflect on their work and to ask questions; and so on.

Figure 5.6   Sample Rubric for the Lesson

PERFORMANCE OBJECTIVE

The student will read the story, *The Last Ride of Molly.* The student will list two brave things that the author of the story did. Then the student will write an expository paragraph on the following topic: "People show they are brave in many ways. Choose *one* time when you were brave or someone else was brave. This other person might be a character in a story, a historical figure, a relative, or a present-day hero. Name the person, if it is not you, and describe what happened."

The student will read the finished paragraph aloud to the class.

DETAILED DESCRIPTION

Students will use the attached rubric.

Time to Complete: 2 days

The student will do the following:

1. List two brave things the author of the short story did.
2. Write an expository paragraph naming a brave person and describing the incident.
3. Read the paragraph aloud to the class using appropriate tone and pacing.

GENERAL CRITERIA

- Follow directions involving time and format.
- Use a logical sequence of development.
- Use correct mechanics (i.e., spelling, punctuation, capitalization).
- Use complete sentences. Vary the length and type of sentences.
- Read the paragraph aloud to the class using appropriate tone and pacing.

ENGLISH LANGUAGE ARTS STANDARDS STRESSED

- Standard: Students will make oral presentations that demonstrate appropriate consideration of the audience, purpose, and the information to be conveyed.
- Standard: Students will identify the basic facts and main ideas in a text and use them as the basis of interpretation.
- Standard: Students will identify, analyze, and apply knowledge of theme in a literary work and provide evidence to support their understanding.
- Standard: Students will plan and present readings, recitations, and performances that demonstrate appropriate consideration of audience and purpose.
- Standard: Students will write with focus, coherent organization, and sufficient detail.
- Standard: Students will use knowledge of standard English conventions in their writing.

SAMPLE RUBRIC FOR THE LESSON

TOPIC DEVELOPMENT	4	3	2	1
Use of Topic Sentence	*Exceptional* Topic sentence is clear, pointed.	*Good* Topic sentence is clear.	*Satisfactory* There is a topic sentence.	*Incomplete* There is no topic sentence.
Use of Supporting Details	*Rich* Paragraph uses many details found in the story.	*Sufficient* Paragraph uses some details found in the story.	*Adequate* Paragraph uses at least two details.	*Lacking* Paragraph uses no details from the story.
Use of Expanded Details	*Rich* Paragraph uses many details from other stories.	*Strong* Paragraph uses some details from other stories.	*Limited* Paragraph uses one detail from other stories.	*Lacking* Paragraph uses no details from other stories.
Use of Concluding Sentence	*Effective* Sums up all points being made in a new way.	*Sufficient* Sums up all points being made.	*Satisfactory* Sums up some points.	*Lacking* No concluding sentence.

(Continued)

Figure 5.6 (Continued)

ENGLISH CONVENTIONS	4	3	2	1
Punctuation (commas, end marks)	Excellent Correct use of periods, question marks, and commas in a series all the time.	Effective Correct use of periods, question marks all of the time and commas in a series most of the time.	Insufficient Correct use of periods and question marks all of the time and commas in a series some of the time.	Lacking Correct use of periods and question marks most of the time but no use of commas in a series.
Spelling	Exceptional No errors.	Effective Two or less errors.	Adequate Four or less errors.	Needs Work More than four errors.
Varied Sentences (used varied beginnings)	Exceptional All varied sentences.	Effective Some varied sentences.	Inadequate Few varied sentences.	Lacking No varied sentences.
Complete Sentences	Exceptional No errors.	Effective Only one fragment.	Adequate Two or less fragments.	Needs Work More than two fragments.
Capital Letters (use of I, first letter in a sentence, and proper nouns)	Exceptional No errors.	Effective Two or less errors.	Ineffective Three or four errors.	Needs Work More than four errors.

ORAL PRESENTATION	4	3	2	1
Voice (tone: pitch, emphasis, pronunciation)	Fluid Even pitch, stress on all key words, correct pronunciation.	Effective Even pitch, stress on most key words, mostly correct pronunciation.	Varied Uneven pitch, stress on some key words, basic pronunciation.	Monotone Boring pitch, no stress on key words, awkward pronunciation.
Pacing (speed of delivery)	Excellent Pacing commands audience's attention.	Effective Pacing is effective in keeping audience's attention.	Unsteady Either is too fast or too slow; barely holds audience's attention.	Weak Goes from too fast to too slow; doesn't hold audience's attention.
Body Language/Eye Contact	Strong Commands audience's attention.	Effective Holds audience's attention.	Inadequate Barely holds audience's attention.	Needs Work Doesn't hold audience's attention.

TOTAL POINTS	

Point Totals	Status
48–43 Points	Advanced
42–37 Points	Proficient
36–31 Points	Passing
30–12 Points	Needs Improvement

Many rubrics are available on the Internet, in educational texts, and from colleagues, which deal with every conceivable subject area. Many sites have rubric generators that ask the teacher to list the criteria that the site then uses to create a personalized rubric. Rather than trying to reinvent the wheel, teachers should use these resources by modifying them to meet the specifics they require. If none of the premade rubrics fulfills the specific needs of a lesson, the teacher should consider the following steps in creating a new rubric.

Resources available to write rubrics.

- Have students brainstorm ways to judge what a successfully completed task should look like. What do you want students to know and be able to do? These are the criteria.

- Group these brainstormed ideas around common descriptors (punctuation, spelling, sentence structure might group around the category English Conventions).

- Describe a range of attributes (start from the undeveloped and proceed to the most successful).

- Write your high range descriptors first (these are actually the goals for the learning).

- Write your low range descriptors next (these will be the problem areas).

- Write the middle range of descriptors last.

- Select a format (usually a grid).

- Label each of the parts and assign your code, which is usually a number range for the levels of performance going from 4 (Mastery) down to 1 (Needs Work).

- Field test the rubric and revise as necessary.

- If students have not been involved in the creation process, make sure they understand all of the components and requirements of the rubric.

The rubric in Figure 5.7 has been designed to assess all rubrics that a teacher either creates from scratch or modifies from the Web. By looking at the necessary criteria and levels of performance, a teacher should be able to determine whether the new rubric addresses the needs of the students, as well as those of the performance objective. In short, assess what you have created.

Rubrics don't always have to be written using a four-column structure. Depending on the project or the activity, they can also be written as a two-column grid representing criteria in one column and a level of performance in the other (see Figure 5.11). This is generally a relatively easy structure to compose and use to determine progress toward a goal.

The use of assessments helps to create active learners who can see progress, adjust performance, and achieve success. Teachers need to become more proactive in requesting time and space in order to share assessments and strategies with their peers. Similarly, teachers should not just rely on a single assessment type but should select the format that can provide the best information to the teacher and especially to the student.

Figure 5.7 Rubric Assessment

CRITERIA	4	3	2	1
Thinking Skills	Complex task involving higher order thinking skills.	Less complicated task involving mid-level thinking skills.	Simpler task involving mid-level thinking skills.	Simple task involving low-level thinking skills.
Goals	Clearly stated and reachable.	A little ambiguous but reachable.	A little ambiguous and not all goals are reachable.	Unclear, unreachable, and not realistic.
Range	Clearly describes criteria across a range of abilities.	Partially describes criteria across a range of abilities.	Range delineations are vague.	Does not describe a range.
Measurability	Criteria are observable and measurable.	Most criteria are observable.	Only a few criteria are observable.	Criteria are unobservable and nonmeasurable.
Age Appropriateness	Criteria are appropriate to the grade level but encourage enrichment.	Most criteria are appropriate to the grade level.	Some criteria are appropriate to the grade level.	Criteria are below grade level.
Vocabulary	Wording is appropriate to the students.	Most wording is appropriate to the students.	Some wording is inappropriate to the students.	Most wording is inappropriate to the students.
Attitude	All levels of performance stated in positive terms.	Most levels of performance stated in positive terms.	Some levels of performance stated in positive terms.	Levels of performance stated only in negative terms.

Figure 5.8 Sample Reading Rubric

CRITERIA	4	3	2	1
Reading Strategies	Independently can apply all reading strategies.	Independently can apply most reading strategies.	Independently can apply some reading strategies.	Can apply some reading strategies with teacher's help.
Fluency	Above grade-level standard with 90% accuracy.	At grade-level standard with 90% accuracy.	Grade-level standard with 80% + accuracy.	Grade appropriate standard with less than 80% accuracy.
Reading Comprehension	Reads for meaning using a variety of above grade-level reading materials.	Reads for meaning using many grade-level reading materials.	Reads at grade level using some materials.	Needs adult support to read near grade level.
Range of Texts	Reads more than 25 books per school year.	Reads 25 books per school year.	Reads fewer than 25 books per year.	Reads few books through the year.

Figure 5.9   Sample English Language Arts Rubric

CRITERIA	4	3	2	1
Sentence Structure	Lack of sentence fragments.	No more than one sentence fragment.	No more than two sentence fragments.	Uncontrolled sentence structure.
Subject-Verb Agreement	Excellent	Effective	Adequate	Ineffective
Capitalization	Correct use.	Effective use.	Adequate use.	Ineffective use.
Punctuation	Correct use of commas, end marks, semicolons, apostrophes, quotation marks, and underlining.	Effective use of commas, end marks, semicolons, apostrophes, quotation marks, and underlining.	Weak use of commas, end marks, semicolons, apostrophes, quotation marks, and underlining.	Uncontrolled use or lack of use of commas, end marks, semicolons, apostrophes, quotation marks, and underlining.
Spelling	Correct use of spelling.	Two or fewer spelling errors.	Three spelling errors.	Needs work.

FROM STANDARD TO ASSESSMENT

Figure 5.12 shows how to start with the standard, unlock it (break it up into meaningful, easily understandable parts), create performance objectives based on each of the parts, and devise assessment pieces to go with them. By following the steps, the teacher can write the standards in grade-appropriate language and post them in the classroom for easy reference by the students.

WHAT MOST PEOPLE NEED TO KNOW

Middle managers must help teachers to collect, share, and use assessment resources. The more the task of designing assessment pieces becomes a shared activity among teachers, their colleagues, and the students, the quicker positive results will appear. The key is for middle management to do the following:

- Secure the time and place where teachers have the opportunity to work together developing common assessments.
- Provide an easily accessible file or written collection of formative assessment resources that are created and can be used by all of the teachers.
- Encourage teachers to post their rubrics on the Web to assist parents to provide home tutoring.
- Poll the staff on their need for necessary professional development programs on assessment practices.

(Text continues on page 57)

Figure 5.10 Sample Mathematics Rubric

CRITERIA	ADVANCED	AT GRADE LEVEL	NEEDS IMPROVEMENT
Understanding the Concept	Reworked the problem into the appropriate mathematical concepts, chose the important data from the problem, and used diagrams or symbols to represent parts of the problem.	Showed partial understanding of the appropriate mathematical concepts, chose some of the important data from the problem, and used some diagrams or symbols.	Showed limited understanding of the appropriate mathematical concepts; used nonrelevant data from the problem, and used some nonrelevant diagrams or symbols.
Applying Mathematical Procedures	Used appropriate procedures to solve the problem correctly.	Solved part of the problem (an error in computation).	Used inappropriate procedures to arrive at an incorrect solution (multiple computation errors).
Interpreting the Results	Used a mathematical strategy that was consistent with the requirements posed by the question.	Used a strategy that was only partially consistent with the requirements posed by the question.	Used a strategy that was unrelated to the requirements posed by the question.
Communicating the Reasoning and the Results	Used mathematical vocabulary and appropriate visual aids (charts, graphs, etc.) to communicate the reasoning behind the correct solution.	Used some mathematical vocabulary that was unclear; used some visual aids that were unclear; did not fully explain the reasoning behind the correct solution.	Used few mathematical terms or used them incorrectly; used no visual aids or used them incorrectly; did not clearly explain the reasoning; provided an incorrect solution.

Figure 5.11 Sample Participation Rubric

CRITERIA	LEVEL OF PERFORMANCE
Student is consistently helping to lead class discussion and is using inferencing, application, and evaluation skills within each class period.	ADVANCED
Student is usually initiating questions and framing responses multiple times within each class period.	ABOVE GRADE LEVEL
The student occasionally responds to questions but not with consistency or frequency.	AT GRADE LEVEL
The student rarely responds to questions and is often distracted or a distraction.	NEEDS IMPROVEMENT

Figure 5.12   Sample: From Standard to Assessment

STANDARD
Grade 3 . . . Standard 10: Genre "Students will identify, analyze, and apply knowledge of the characteristics of different genres (Distinguish among forms of literature such as poetry, fiction, nonfiction, and drama)."

Take the standard and unlock what it requires.

UNLOCKING THE STANDARD	
KEY ADJECTIVES/NOUNS	**VERBS**
Students	identify
knowledge	analyze
characteristics	apply
different genres (poetry, fiction, nonfiction, drama)	

Use the key adjectives, nouns, and verbs to tell you what students should know and be able to do.

WHAT WILL STUDENTS BE ABLE TO DO AS A RESULT OF KNOWING THE STANDARD?
1. They will be able to identify the characteristics of poetry.
2. They will be able to analyze the characteristics of poetry.
3. They will be able to use the characteristics to write poetry.
4. They will be able to identify the characteristics of fiction.
5. They will be able to analyze the characteristics of fiction.
6. They will be able to use the characteristics to create fiction pieces.
7. They will be able to identify the characteristics of nonfiction.
8. They will be able to analyze the characteristics of nonfiction.
9. They will be able to use the characteristics to create nonfiction pieces.
10. They will be able to identify the characteristics of drama.
11. They will be able to analyze the characteristics of drama.
12. They will be able to use the characteristics to create short drama pieces.

Now create performance objectives.

PERFORMANCE OBJECTIVE 1
CONDITION: Using the two poems students wrote in class . . .
TASK: . . . the student will be able to identify the characteristics of poetry . . .
CRITERIA: . . . by defining and giving an example of rhyme, rhythm, stanza, and line break.

(Continued)

Figure 5.12 (Continued)

PERFORMANCE OBJECTIVE 2
CONDITION: Using the two poems students wrote in class . . .
TASK: . . . the student will be able to analyze the characteristics of poetry . . .
CRITERIA: . . . by identifying the end rhyme scheme as **aa, bb, cc** or as **ab, ab, cd, cd.**

Take the criteria from the performance objective and create a rubric that may be used to assess student progress toward mastery.

PERFORMANCE OBJECTIVE 1

CRITERIA	4	3	2	1
Rhyme	Define and give an example in both poems.	Define and give an example in one of the poems.	Either define or give an example in at least one poem.	Unable to define or give example in either poem.
Rhythm	Define and give an example in both poems.	Define and give an example in one of the poems.	Either define or give an example in at least one poem.	Unable to define or give example in either poem.
Stanza	Define and give an example in both poems.	Define and give an example in one of the poems.	Either define or give an example in at least one poem.	Unable to define or give example in either poem.
Line Break	Define and give an example in both poems.	Define and give an example in one of the poems.	Either define or give an example in at least one poem.	Unable to define or give example in either poem.

PERFORMANCE OBJECTIVE 2

CRITERIA	4	3	2	1
AA, BB, CC	Can identify end rhyme scheme in both poems.	Can identify end rhyme scheme in one poem.	Can identify end rhyme scheme with assistance.	Is unable to identify end rhyme scheme in either poem.
AB, AB, CD, CD	Can identify end rhyme scheme in both poems.	Can identify end rhyme scheme in one poem.	Can identify end rhyme scheme with assistance.	Is unable to identify end rhyme scheme in either poem.

- Monitor and check to see that formative assessments are being used by all the teachers all the time.
- Provide teachers with feedback on their use of formative assessment practices.

WHAT SOME PEOPLE NEED TO KNOW

Administrators need to be aware that performance assessments are one of the main driving cogs in the education wheel. They provide the data in the classroom, as well as from the classroom, that drives decision making at all levels. Students need the data to be able to revise their work in progress; teachers need it to adjust the lesson strategies; middle managers need it for accountability of the learning taking place; and top level administrators need it to provide budgetary focus where it will have the most impact. Even parents need it at all levels in order to support the students, as well as the educational aims of the district. Part of the assessment process involves communicating the status of the learner to the parents. Administrators should apprise the teachers, students, and parents of the need for a standards-based reporting system that transcends grades in lieu of meaningful information on the learning status and ongoing progress of the learner.

SUMMARY

To create a standards-based education system, one of the primary focus points needs to be in the area of assessment, specifically formative assessment. Positive strides may be taken by providing students and teachers with those precise criteria against which to judge success and growth. Both teachers and students benefit most when the following strategies are used to provide the data that is necessary to alter and adjust.

- Observations
- Models
- Exemplars
- Narratives
- Checklists
- Rubrics

6 Data

People who take pride in seeing how many groceries they can get with the least amount of money are, in actuality, the greatest data collectors and organizers of all. Not only do they have to secure the coupons from a variety of sources, but they also have to create expiration schedules, match products with family needs, allocate storage space for consumables, gather recipes to correspond with the sale items, research times when the product is on sale to maximize the benefits of the rebate, and a whole lot of other extraordinary functions. Only then are they featured in a tabloid under the heading "I Fed a Family of Four for Six Years for Three Cents a Day." These people create filing systems that would boggle the Pentagon, and they can reference the date that a can of creamed corn, which normally sells for 59 cents, can be purchased for a penny with the additional prize of a free box of instant rice as a promotion. Shoeboxes serve to hold alphabetized rows of coupons for use in the stores, while computers chronicle the purchase and savings differences. These people collect and use data to make informed choices that they feel will benefit their families. The same process (collect, analyze, apply) is now being used in the educational environment.

State frameworks set into place the same conditions: collect and use data to make informed decisions about the educational welfare of students. These standards create the final outcome for each grade level in a school and establish timelines for moving all children to the level of proficiency or beyond. In this scenario, assessments are administered and corrected by the states, the data is analyzed, adequate yearly progress (AYP) is established, and the results are returned to the local agencies so the schools and districts have the information necessary to answer the following questions.

- How far have we progressed?
- In what areas are our students having difficulty?
- What specific students are having difficulty?
- What changes need to be made in our teaching?

In addition, if districts create local benchmark assessments (formative), they will generate more precise information, which helps to identify the curriculum gaps of students. This data will enable teachers to better identify and address the root of the problems that affect student learning.

There are three data sources. The first is the standardized testing data compiled by federal or state government agencies, arranged, and fed back to the school districts in order to raise the general performance level of students. Numerous statistics involving age, race, income level, ethnic background, and the like are included, along with a breakdown of the test results. While individual scores may be addressed, there is a collective mentality, involving moving groups of students to achieve at a higher level.

The second source is data from the district that identifies areas of interest, usually by grade level. Pretesting or posttesting results are often figured, and assumptions involving general curriculum adjustments are discussed. The data is often used to promote grade-level decision making. And the last source is data in an individual classroom that is compiled by a teacher. This information is used to make adjustments involving the performance of individual students. While the first and second types of data will be discussed more fully in future publications, the focus in this text is on the classroom use.

WHAT IS DATA AND FROM WHERE DOES IT COME?

Data is factual evidence of the degree to which something has been learned and applied (for example, 96% of all students got problem 6 correct on the final exam; Johnny got 9 out of 10 questions right on a fractions quiz; Mary received 14 out of a possible 16 points in a scoring rubric on mechanics on her paper on digestive disorders). Data can be observed and measured.

Data may come from a variety of sources.

- *Application data* describes the degree to which a student or group of students has performed in becoming proficient or mastering specific knowledge and skills as they apply to standards.
  - o Teacher-created tests or standardized tests (summative)
  - o Demonstrations, visual or oral presentations
  - o Projects
  - o Performance assessments (formative)
  - o Reports, essays, term papers
- *Methods data* communicates how the teacher makes decisions about curriculum, assessment, instruction, and resources.
- *Background data* identifies factors that assist the teacher in understanding the students and their unique needs.
  - o Primary language
  - o Special programs
  - o Attendance
  - o English language proficiency

THE STANDARDS-BASED MODEL AND DATA

In the past, data has often been collected to measure and report in the form of a letter grade. Little has been done with the data from assessments to be prescriptive, to improve student learning through the change in teaching practices. In the standards-based model, the intent of using data is twofold. First, it is used to find the gaps in learning and to modify the teaching in order to improve the learning of all students. Second, data is used specifically to demonstrate to parents the progress their children have made toward achievement of the state and local standards.

Although some people might criticize the standards-based model and complain that it takes away the freedom of the teacher to be creative, in reality, this is merely misplaced criticism. The standards-based model does not limit or stifle a teacher's ability to be creative at all. What it does, however, is to outline the parameters and maintain the pathway of all students toward achievement of specific standards. Teachers still have the ability to be creative in the development of activities in the process of teaching. In fact, teachers can and must be more creative in the process of developing instruction to meet the individual needs of all students. If districts create standardized benchmark assessments and continually examine the data to measure progress toward mastery of the standards, teachers can find the curriculum gaps, make valid comparisons of student performance, and modify the delivery of content to maintain a true trajectory toward the intended target.

WHAT EVERYONE NEEDS TO KNOW

Certain basic questions need to be asked for people to understand the role of data in classroom assessment.

- Which students are not successful?
- What are the specific areas in which students have weaknesses in knowledge or skills?
- Do all students have the same high expectations?
- Are the assessments consistent for all students?
- Are the standards being addressed for all students?
- Is the delivery of instruction meeting the needs of all of the students?

Teachers need to be aware that ongoing assessment of students will produce information that should identify the areas of strength as well as the needs of an individual student's understanding and application of the standards.

FORM VERSUS FUNCTION

With most word processing programs, manufacturers have built-in data presentation devices (pie, bubble, 3-D, bar, column, cone, pyramid, and cylinder charts are but a few). They can be printed in colors, shades, and sizes. For presentation to administrators, school committees, or state departments of education, they are extremely effective. These are the *form* presentations. But, they often aren't meant to give timely information (that which can be used to make adjustments in an ongoing process); therefore, they are often after-the-fact pieces that allow changes for the next but not present stakeholders. Teachers need something for today, the *function* resources. They need data that can be used "now" and a format that makes it meaningful.

Craig Jerald, in his article "Cooking With Data" (2003), says that words get in the way for educators to use data in the classroom. Many teachers and administrators never had sufficient courses or training in the collection, sorting, and application of data. They look at the terms, such as *disaggregate,* as frightening and confusing. People who have limited number-sense often would rather ignore data statistics than face being exposed as unprepared. Adding and dividing the numbers in a grade book to get a grade is all they want to do. Likewise, collecting and sorting data can help to identify problems, but this also implies the necessity to create solutions. In certain instances, this takes educators out of their comfort zone and produces introspection that may not be easy to address.

SIMPLICITY IS THE KEY

If something isn't easy, people avoid it; therefore, to identify, collect, and analyze data, a teacher has to know where and how to start.

- *Step 1: Asking the Important Question (IQ).* It is the question about essential aspects of a student, in relationship to the desired skill necessary to achieve proficiency or mastery in a standard. If answered, this will inform the teacher about which actions to take to close the gap between the student's present level of achievement and the desired level of achievement. Good IQ should involve the following:
  - o The IQ identifies a matter that relates to improving teaching and learning.
  - o The IQ can open an inquiry process in which the collection and analysis of data can help in finding a solution.
  - o The solution will have meaning to the teacher and the learner.
  - o The solution will be used.

If the teacher already knows the answer (there is no data, hope, or desire to use the solution), then common sense dictates that a person doesn't have the important question properly framed. Here are some sample IQs that could lead to positive results:

  - o Why can't a majority of students in my class convert fractions into decimals?
  - o Why can't Tom write a complete sentence when describing a math solution, although he can when writing an expository paragraph in English language arts?
  - o Why did half the students check answer B on question 6 of the multiple-choice test when the correct answer was C?
  - o Why do 25% of students in my class use *there-they're-there, too-to, know-no, your-you're, its-it's,* and *then-than* interchangeably in their writing?

- *Step 2: Identify the data.* What types of data will be used to assist in formulating a conclusion. Don't restrict yourself with too little data, as that will slant the conclusion. Likewise, don't overwhelm yourself with so much data that the analysis phase will require a team of consultants. Will you use the latest tests, quizzes, observation narratives, and so on? These are choices the teacher must make in trying to get pertinent data. Now you can collect it.

- *Step 3: Organize the data.* Sort it (that's what *disaggregate* means), so you can break it down into manageable small groups or categories that you can quickly understand. Here are some examples:
  - Male versus female students
  - Students who use graphic organizers versus students who don't
  - Students who score higher on multiple-choice tests versus students who score higher on writing assignments
  - Students who got problem 6 wrong, students who got problem 8 wrong, students who got problem 11 wrong

- *Step 4: Analyze the data.* Look for trends or patterns that relate to the IQ. Compare multiple pieces of data to each other.

- *Step 5: Draw conclusions.* Don't make a summary of the data; see how it relates to the IQ. Don't make assumptions. Go where the data leads you, not where you want the data to go.

- *Step 6: Implement solutions.* Base the implementation plan on the conclusion. Weigh which solutions will have the most immediate impact and implement those first.

A teacher in a New Hampshire high school saw that student scores in her class were dropping in math almost across the board. The teacher took the results of the last test and made a simple form composed of two columns labeled WHICH ONES DID YOU GET WRONG and WHICH ONES WERE THE EASIEST (these were the important questions) and handed one to each student. After handing back the tests, the teacher asked each student to fill out the form anonymously and hand it back (this was identifying the data). That done, the instructor had one student take the completed forms to the board and transpose the answers on a mock-up form the teacher had drawn; it replicated the form the students had used (this is organizing the data). The data was now there for everyone to see. The next question the teacher asked was, "Now is there anything we can see from these results?" (this is analyzing the data). Hands popped up and students responded.

- "Most of us answered the first four questions correctly, but we screwed up on problems 5, 6, and 8."

- "Problems 6 and 8 appear to be the ones most people had difficulty with."

- "We got 1 through 4, and 9 and 10, but 5, 6, and 8 were the toughest. Problem 7, about 50% got it right."

The teacher then said, "What conclusions can you draw from this?" (this is drawing conclusions). After a few moments, hands started to raise again.

- "We need more work on those types of problems. We don't understand what those problems were asking."
- "We spent too much time in class going over stuff we already could do. We need to spend more time learning and practicing this stuff we didn't get."
- "We spend too much time in class reviewing homework from last night. We need time in class to practice things we learned."

The teacher said, "How are we going to do this?" Again, hands flew into the air.

- "Less homework. Then we don't have to spend time reviewing it and we can practice what we need to practice."
- "More group time. That way we can get help from each other if we're having trouble."
- "You have to give us more examples so we can understand it better."
- "Those questions on the test weren't fair. We really didn't spend enough time in class going over the material. You shouldn't give us homework to do that covers things we really haven't learned in class."
- "We need to pay more attention in class."

Upon hearing the responses, the teacher walked over to the list of problems she had assigned for homework and halved them. She then facilitated selection of groups that would tackle each of the troublesome test problems the next day (this is implementing solutions). The students came in the next day eager to begin. As stakeholders, they knew their voices had meaning and that they were responsible for implementing some of the solutions. This was pretty simple, but it had an impact on their learning. The template in Figure 6.1 is designed to assist teachers in stating the problem, asking the important question, organizing the data, drawing conclusions, and finding solutions.

At times, data from outside of the classroom may be introduced to provide a clearer picture as to a student's difficulties. For example, George was having problems completing some homework assignments, and his performance on certain tests was well below his normal average. Yet, on other days, he responded with great success in applying those same skills. The data seemed to indicate that tests and homework assignments on Tuesdays and Thursdays were lowest, while Monday, Wednesday, and Friday, George did exceptionally well. Since nothing in the present data could explain this aberration, another data source was needed. On examination, the teacher discovered that George's mother and father both worked in their convenience store on Monday and Wednesday nights, but only the father worked all week. On those nights, George spent his time in the store until closing, 11:00 PM, doing odd jobs. Both his disassociation from homework and his lack of preparation on those nights contributed to his

Figure 6.1   Sample Data Template

Problem	More than a third of the students in my third period class are unable to write a coherent thesis statement as required by Standard 12 in English Language Arts.
Important Question	Why are so many of my students unable to write a coherent thesis statement?
Data Source	Essays from 12/1, 12/9, and 12/14.
D A T A	6 students had an incomplete thesis statement on all three essays. 8 students had incomplete thesis statements on at least two essays. 4 students had no thesis statements on all three essays. 5 students had no thesis statements on at least two essays. Only 4 students out of the entire class could define *thesis statement* when I asked each person individually. 3 students who wrote successful thesis statements told me they lucked out and really weren't sure how they did it. 10 students did not develop all of the points in their thesis statements. 7 students wrote successful thesis statements, which they developed in their essays.

ORGANIZING THE DATA			
Category 1 *Title* Total Success	Category 2 *Title* >50% Success	Category 3 *Title* <49% Success	Category 4 *Title* Lost Souls
7 students wrote successful thesis statements.	3 students wrote successful thesis by luck.	5 students had no thesis on at least two essays.	6 students had incomplete thesis all three essays.
4 students could define thesis statement.		10 students didn't develop all points.	4 students no thesis all three essays.
		8 students had undeveloped points on at least two essays.	

Analysis	Only 4 students out of 24 could define thesis. Only 7 students out of 24 wrote successful thesis statements. One-fourth of the students in the class had incomplete thesis statements on all three essays. One-third of the students had incomplete thesis statements on at least two essays. A little over one-fifth of the students had no thesis statements on all three essays.
Conclusions	The vast majority of the students in the class don't really know what a thesis statement is. Only a small fraction of students are successful in writing and developing thesis statements.
Solutions	The teacher has to reteach the concept of the thesis sentence before assigning essays. The teacher must explore methodology other than that used the previous time. The teacher has to provide more exemplars. The teacher should provide more guided practice on thesis statements. The rubrics for assessment aren't specific enough, are too extensive and don't address this issue, have no ownership to the students, or are misunderstood. The teacher shouldn't go on to full essays until the skill involving thesis statements is established. The teacher needs to differentiate the lessons so that students in each category can proceed at a their own growth pace, from enrichment for those who "got it" to basic strategies for those who are unsuccessful. The teacher should consider additional scaffolding strategies. The teacher should consider grouping strategies to use the talents of the students who already can do it.

lack of success in school the next day. On days when his mother was home and provided him with direction, and he had an earlier curfew, he succeeded in school the next day. Armed with the data, the teacher contacted George's parents hoping they might have an answer. They saw the factual evidence and arranged for an aunt to take care of George on those two nights. Almost immediately, George's performance rose to the satisfaction of the teacher, George, and his parents.

STUDENT PORTFOLIOS

Student portfolios are important in the standards-based process. They provide teachers with a place to hold data for future reference, and create a long-term and short-term look at a student's specific progress and achievement toward mastery of the standards. Portfolios also provide an opportunity for students, teachers, and parents to reflect on the quality of work at any given time. The following list serves to identify the specific benefits of portfolios.

- Identify student progress in relationship to the standards.
- Create an opportunity for reflection upon the work.
- Justify and document curricular modifications within the classroom to accommodate individual student needs.
- Demonstrate student performance for administration and parents.
- Create a record of what has been done to date.
- Give students an opportunity to take responsibility for learning.
- Give students the opportunity to take ownership in their learning process.

The portfolio checklist in Figure 6.2 is an example of a tool that teachers can place in the front of each student portfolio to identify what has been included. This checklist may also serve as a reference to identify what documents need to be included.

WHAT MOST PEOPLE NEED TO KNOW

Data plays a significant role in the process of finding the gaps in curriculum and instruction because without it, the pathway for student achievement may vary, stop, or even regress. The responsibility of the directors, department chairs, curriculum coordinators, facilitators, and assistant principals is to manage time created by the central office to organize the teaching staff and facilitate meetings to establish a process for the collection and analysis of data. They also must be held accountable to deliver and maintain quality control of data used to determine a direct, continuous pathway for student achievement. The following list contains some examples of the strategies that middle-level managers would facilitate and implement in the standards-based model.

Figure 6.2 Portfolio Checklist

Student Name _____	**Grade** _____

_____ Student performance records on all state assessments.

_____ Quarterly report card that identifies the degree of achievement a student has made toward the standards. This may be in the form of a continuum line or a narrative.

_____ Attendance record.

_____ Writing samples.

_____ Samples of student work that demonstrate student knowledge and development of language and reading skills.

_____ Samples of math work that demonstrate sequencing and improvement.

_____ Samples of work that demonstrate chronological student progress throughout each year in subjects other than reading and math.

_____ Signed and dated copies of the local grade-level expectations that were given to parents and students.

- Organize staff around an ongoing assessment process.

- Develop and implement the assessment process.

- Organize staff to develop tests, quizzes, graphic organizers, templates, and rubrics based on multiple learning styles.

- Coordinate the collection and analysis of data and a student portfolio system that is consistent throughout the school.

- Ensure the modification of curriculum and instruction to meet individual student needs.

- Implement a student assistance program.

- Develop the plan to report results of data and the progress of students to parents.

- Coordinate and ensure quality time for teachers to analyze data.

- Create a data collection system to ensure a safe and drug free school.

WHAT SOME PEOPLE NEED TO KNOW

In the pyramid of responsibility (see Chapter 1), the individuals at the top have the greatest responsibility for the content of No Child Left Behind. School committee members, superintendents, and principals must be fully aware of all facets of the law to ensure compliance and implementation. As overseers, they must also be able to delegate responsibility and develop accountability systems to assure that compliance remains at the correct levels. Yet, with respect to data, these system managers do not necessarily need to know "how" as much as they need to know "what." As middle managers are the button pushers of the system that keep it going, the administrators are the finger pointers that drive the system forward. They are the individuals that ask the questions: What are the systems in place for the collection of data? Where is the data? What does it demonstrate? What is the root of the problem? What changes have been or need to be made to address the learning gaps? The answers to these questions provide them with the direction to take, to move the district or individual schools forward.

SUMMARY

Data is an essential part of a standards-based system, since it's what drives monitoring and adjusting on the part of the students and the teacher. It is used to find the gaps in learning and to keep students and parents informed about the progress toward achieving the standards. It answers the following questions in regard to student performance:

- How far has the student progressed?
- In what areas is the student having difficulty?
- What specific students are having difficulty?
- What changes need to be made in the teaching?

The three types of data—application data, methods data, and background data—provide distinct lenses to look at students and the learning process. Simplicity is the key to using data in the classroom.

7 Unit Design

O ne of the many traits of human beings is that they have a tendency to proceed faster than conditions allow. Sometimes they impose this need for speed on themselves, and other times they are given timetables that are difficult or even impossible to meet. For example, has anyone ever read the instruction manual that comes with a new computer? Who has ever read all of the pages in the manual for programming a TV? Yet that doesn't stop people from using these devices. It does, however, illustrate the point that only when people get stuck do they take the time to address the steps necessary to solve a problem.

Education is much the same way. In the past, many systems dumped a "curriculum" on teachers, told them where the book and supply closets were, and left them to put everything together. Time was always an enemy since teachers, right or wrong, had the expectation they had to finish all the "curriculum" that was on their plate. The educational buffet appeared endless, so they were forced to pick and choose, hoping that at the end they had saved enough time for the truly worthwhile items. All too often, though, the tray held equal amounts of rudimentary staples and ancillary side dishes. Unfortunately, they got stuck; there was no time to go back to see where basic items needed to be inserted and reinforced. Instead, teachers rationalized their lack of success by saying that the next time around, they would devote more time and energy to specific essential areas. But they were doomed from the beginning because *curriculum* is too broad to interpret; only *standards* are specific.

In essence, the whole process was like trying to build a house on quicksand; after the teacher thought that the foundation was fairly set and was ready to go on, the basement disappeared below the surface. Not wishing to give up on the work that had been done, the teacher continued to erect the first then the second floors only to see them also slip beneath the sand, all the time hoping there was an end. The system, in trying to help, then had more teachers adding more floors hoping that some might remain above ground, but the sinking often continued because the foundation, if it existed, was shaky since it wasn't clearly defined.

The old bridge is sinking, and so is the old educational system. The classic film *The Bridge on the River Kwai* clearly demonstrates this. After numerous unsuccessful attempts by his engineers, the Japanese commander must turn to his British prisoners for help in erecting the bridge that his superiors have commanded him to build. The first thing the British do is to test the river bottom, discovering that the Japanese had begun construction on a bottomless pit of sandy bottom. The prisoners assume total control, move the site, create directed-work crews, and build a masterful bridge. The British set standards first: anchor the foundation on rock.

The traditional education problem was simple: the system took a number of teachers at the same grade level, gave them the same books and supplies, then let them pick out what they felt was important to teach. There often was little time in the day for collaboration. Students from Teacher A might never get the emphasis that Teacher B gave. Teacher C might decide to spend more or less time on a content area than Teacher D. At the end of the year, students were in various places in the "curriculum." The next year, these students were now heterogeneously grouped so there were pupils at a variety of skill levels all in the same class. Teacher A's students were proceeding successfully while Teacher D's students were struggling. These new grade-level teachers (E, F, G, and H) were also confronted with the same problems as their predecessors: time and content. So, the problem became compounded every year, and the students and teachers became frustrated. An easy way to verify this is to go to any school system and speak to the fourth grade teachers. They can identify which teachers their students had in the past without ever looking up the records. Not only do they know where the deficiencies lie, but they can trace the roots of student success and failure. And, more often than not, they are expected to fix the problem now with their present students rather than at the source, so catch-up becomes the substitute for education.

UNITS CREATE FOCUS

Most books are divided into chapters, which serve multiple purposes: they allow a continuity of events, they give the brain an opportunity to accept newly introduced characters, and they provide time for reflection on plot and theme. These units (chapters) create a whole entity that has a clear and direct focus. They take the readers from the beginning of an event and lead them through to a conclusion of sorts. Despite twists and turns, the direction has been clearly plotted, and the reader goes on a controlled journey of discovery. Units in education serve the same purpose. Their function is to provide students with learning opportunities that include times for reflection and application, all in a controlled journey. Think of it as everyone being on an identical bus with an identical driver going to the same location. Time has been built in so that rest stops may vary in length, but each student will see the same sights and hear the same descriptions. The students will be told what to look for in advance. Some drivers may give additional insights, but only when the students can understand them in relationship to the essential materials. At the end of the journey, all of the students can share their similar observations, and some may be able to tell even more about events or sights on the trip. However, there is no guesswork on the destination or on what students are supposed to encounter. And, though they are encouraged to see and hear more, it's not at the expense of the basic information.

For this reason, unit design is essential in a standards-based educational system. Thinking of lessons collectively around a theme, concept, or focus allows the teacher to incorporate multiple standards, a variety of assessments, different learning styles, and opportunities for application of several skills simultaneously.

Teachers can control time on learning more effectively, allowing students an opportunity for reflection. Teachers also can incorporate other subject areas into the unit so that students have more real-world problem-solving experiences. The result is that students get an opportunity to establish connections between their existing knowledge and new information. Activities can also be structured so that students have opportunities to support and learn from others, an essential skill both inside and outside of the classroom.

WHAT EVERYONE NEEDS TO KNOW

The standards for the unit should be clear, stated or written in a grade-appropriate language, delivered to the students before the unit begins, and discussed.

- The students should be told which skills will be learned, how they will be assessed, and how these skills tie into real-world applications.

- The students should be told how each unit ties in with previous learning and how it relates to the next unit, because the brain works best when making connections and finding patterns and purpose.

- The students should be taught the key questions, concepts, and goals to be addressed within each unit.

- The students should be given or assisted in working up a series of organizing questions that allows them to focus on the outcomes and expectations of the unit.

- Students should be provided with the vocabulary necessary for them to understand the new concepts.

- Students should be given the sequence of lessons that comprise the unit, as well as the time allocation for each lesson. These activities should go from the known to the unknown, simple to complex. While time units may be adjusted, the students should work at a comfortable yet productive level.

- Students should be provided with a list or supply of materials, as well as possible resources (such as Internet sites or textbook chapters). Likewise, students should receive a list of technology resources that may assist in the acquisition, completion, or application of the knowledge.

- Students should be informed of the types of assessments to be used. They should be clear in how the assessments will be applied, and they may help in creating rubrics that will be part of the assessment process.

- The teacher needs to build in teaching strategies that take into account the learning and presentation styles of the students. These strategies should build on student strength and ability.

- The learning must be differentiated in order to engage all of the students, and must provide students with the scaffolding or steps necessary to achieve success.

- The teacher should provide focused mini-lessons to explain information, and should model specific knowledge and skills that will be required.

- Exemplars should be used to show students what successful completion of the components of the unit should resemble. The teacher should provide explanations of why, how, and when a skill or strategy is used and should also apply multiple opportunities to use the skills.

- Closure activities not only allow students to demonstrate what they have learned but also help them to reflect on their learning. Keep in mind that reflection is a key that allows the student to establish an ownership of the skill and an understanding of the process in obtaining the skill.

- Opportunities should be provided for the students to practice these skills in real-world problem-solving situations, both in and outside of the classroom.

- Parents must be informed of the goals and expectations of the unit before the start of the activities. The parents should be aware of the standards to be addressed, as well as how the students will be assessed. In addition, the parents should understand how the specific standards fit in to the overall mission statement, as well as the philosophy and objectives of the course and of the school system.

AIDS FOR THE EDUCATOR

One of the most important words in the English language is *planning.* Yet most of us are ambivalent about how to plan. This mainly occurs because some people act in a random fashion, hoping that a design will come forward and give meaning to their actions and decisions. Others are fastidious and plan every decision in meticulous detail, sometimes even paralyzing themselves into inactivity when the slightest thing goes wrong. As a result, this second group cannot adjust, make a decision, or proceed. Luckily, the average person probably fits somewhere in between. Most people have plans for some things but use a "what do you want to do" or "let's see what happens if . . ." strategy for others. A good example might be the fact many people don't really understand the importance of making an outline before they have to write a research paper or a report. Most participants feel the task is time-consuming and interferes with the actual composition. They'd rather just sit down, let the "creative" juices flow, and hope that some sort of organization happens. Once they make an outline, however, they are amazed at the ease of writing. The lesson learned is that planning ultimately saves time and concentrates effort.

Teachers are like the average person. Each day, they are bombarded by various external stimuli that appear to be important, some of which occur inside the classroom and some outside. They are also asked to respond to numerous questions by their students about the activities within their individual worlds. The teachers, though supposed experts in all of their grade-level areas, bring in a series of preferences and skills centered on their specific area of expertise. In short, the teacher would rather do some things and not others. All of these factors influence teacher choices during the presentation of a lesson. If that outline, the definitive plan that ensures that the necessary material will be covered, doesn't exist or is loosely constructed, the teacher can teach "a lesson" but not the "right lesson." Without the unit design, the danger exists that wrong choices can lead to relative and not relevant material being covered.

The average teacher makes thousands of educational decisions a day, and teachers hope the vast majority of these decisions are sound. Yet it's easy to go astray if one depends only on a single day's lesson and doesn't keep the bigger picture in mind. Unit design is the outline, the structure, and the thing that keeps the learning honest and focused. At the same time, it makes daily adjustment easier to handle because the teacher and the students see the overall picture. With proper planning, a bump in the road need not interrupt the scope and sequence.

Students are also beneficiaries of unit design. They can see a pattern to the learning and can more readily grasp the connections between their previous knowledge and the new learning. They are also more prepared to apply the new information to problem-solving situations. While lesson design may focus on practice involving a single standard, with unit design students can see how multiple standards need to be applied to make the unit successful, which is akin to how the students must function in the real world. The learning is, thereby, focused on providing exploration and discovery rather than surprise and shock.

The following templates (see Figures 7.1 through 7.6) are presented to assist teachers in unit design. To be of maximum benefit, a form should also be given to the students and parents in order to foster a learning community. Parents can become resources when they know the expectations, performance objectives, and assessments necessary to measure accomplishment.

The checklist in Figure 7.6 can be used by the teacher to make sure that all of the essential aspects of the lesson have been included.

The teacher form (see Figures 7.1, 7.2) provides a quick way for the educator to monitor the scope and sequence of the unit. Its role also is to keep the lessons focused on relevant as opposed to relative information. Differentiation and enrichment are built in instead of being afterthoughts.

The student and parent form (see Figure 7.5) contains a place for both the student and the parent to sign, indicating that both parties have received the information and are aware of its contents. All parties are then operating with clear goals and expectations, knowing what skills will be developed and how they will be assessed.

One of the most important aspects of unit design is that it allows teachers to incorporate interdisciplinary goals and objectives. This, in turn, allows students to see how learning the standards in one area of study enhances application in others. Furthermore, there are no surprises to students and parents because they are clear about the expectations and the measurements before the unit begins. Students can, therefore, track their own achievement and take corrective measures in a timely and meaningful fashion, thereby making them active, not passive, participants in the education process. And since parents know what is being expected of the students, they can help the students to achieve their goals.

MEASURING SUCCESS

The parent is a critical component in the education community. While this is an easy statement to make, it's often very difficult to understand. So, to simplify

Figure 7.1   Unit Planner—Teacher's Copy (front side)

UNIT PLANNER

UNIT TITLE: **DATE:**

PREVIOUS UNIT: **NEXT UNIT:**

GOAL:

STANDARDS:

ESSENTIAL QUESTIONS:

VOCABULARY:

SEQUENCE OF LESSONS: **TIME SEQUENCE:**

Figure 7.2   Unit Planner—Teacher's Copy (back side)

MATERIALS REQUIRED:	TECHNOLOGY REQUIRED:
ACTIVITIES/APPLICATIONS:	DIFFERENTIATION:
STRATEGIES:	ASSESSMENTS:

Figure 7.3 Unit Planner—Sample Teacher's Copy (front side)

UNIT PLANNER

UNIT TITLE: Weather and You

DATE: November, 2 weeks

PREVIOUS UNIT:
Identifying forms of precipitation

NEXT UNIT:
Animal behavior due to weather

GOAL: Students will be able to chart weather during a particular time in their own community, research weather patterns over the past 10 years, and make trend predictions based on their data charts.

STANDARDS: Making connections to weather in a particular place and time

Collecting and organizing data and identifying appropriate ways to display the data

Identifying and using tools to measure temperature, volume, and speed

ESSENTIAL QUESTIONS:

1. How will you gather data?
2. How will you record data?
3. How will you make a chart?
4. How will you share data?
5. How will you compare present weather patterns to past ones?
6. What will you use as the key factor in making weather predictions?

VOCABULARY: snow, sleet, rain, freezing rain, high pressure, low pressure, gauges, barometer, anemometer, temperature, depth, volume

SEQUENCE OF LESSONS:	TIME SEQUENCE:
1. Understanding the vocabulary	2 days
2. Making our measuring tools, setting up our recording books	Ongoing through 2 weeks
3. Recording the data in our books	3 days
4. Researching weather history for our community	3 days
5. Charting present and past data and sharing the data	3 days
6. Making predictions	2 days

Figure 7.4 Unit Planner—Sample Teacher's Copy (back side)

MATERIALS REQUIRED:
Paper cups, rulers, construction paper, scissors, glue stick, popsicle sticks, pencils, thermometer, measuring cup, pens/markers

TECHNOLOGY REQUIRED:
Internet access to WeatherChannel.com, WeatherClassroom.com, *Farmers' Almanac*, FamilyEducation.com (building a weather station)

ACTIVITIES/APPLICATIONS:

1. Students measure precipitation, wind speed, and temperature (using classroom-made gauges) outside school and their homes, and enter data into record book.
2. Students meet in small groups, share data, and discuss variations.
3. Students go on the Internet or are provided with historical weather data. They record the data in their books.
4. Students chart the present day-to-day data with past information.
5. Students compare the present data to past information and try to draw trend patterns for next November.
6. Students research historical data for the next month and make trend predictions for that month.

DIFFERENTIATION:

1. Students have parents sign up with local radio or television stations to become weather watchers (people who call in daily reports). The students gather the data on a daily basis for the media outlet and keep records to share with the class.
2. Students publish an informational booklet on how to predict weather trends.
3. Students collect data and make regional trend predictions.

STRATEGIES:

1. Use small groups.
2. Allow students to personalize recording devices.
3. Provide time for daily measurement, observation, etc.
4. Check record books often.
5. Create a daily timeline weather chart for use throughout the year.
6. Encourage students to speculate why snow, wind, rain differs in neighborhoods.
7. Provide reflection time so students can formulate patterns.

ASSESSMENTS:

1. Create rubrics with the assistance of the students to check the following:
   if class-made recording devices are accurate,
   if record books are updated daily (accuracy, neatness, etc.),
   if historical data is recorded (accuracy, neatness, etc.),
   if students have shared information with their team,
   if students have charted data correctly,
   if students have identified patterns,
   if student predictions are based on data and observation, etc.

Figure 7.5   Unit Plan—Student and Parent Copy

UNIT PLAN

TEACHER'S NAME:

UNIT TITLE: **DATE:**

GOAL:

STANDARDS:

ESSENTIAL QUESTIONS:

MATERIAL/TECHNOLOGY REQUIREMENTS:

SEQUENCE OF LESSONS:

TIME SEQUENCE:

ASSESSMENTS:

Student's Name: _____

Parent's Signature: _____

Figure 7.6 Unit Planning Checklist

UNIT PLANNING CHECKLIST	YES	NO
Identified the standards to be covered and the skills to be learned.		
Created a need and a real-world reason for students to learn and to apply the new skills.		
Identified introductory activities that tie the new learning to the students' existing knowledge base.		
Sequenced activities appropriately so that lessons provide sufficient scaffolding for all learners.		
Created assessments that are prescriptive and provide relevant feedback for the students to correct and adjust their performance.		
Involved students in helping to create assessment materials.		
Provided lessons that build on the students' strengths and abilities.		
Provided modeling to demonstrate the use of specific knowledge and skills.		
Provided sufficient opportunities for students to practice the skills in as many in-class and outside of class real-world application situations as possible.		
Ensured that students have opportunities to learn from and to support their peers.		
Employed teaching strategies that engage both individual and group learning styles and needs.		
Provided differentiating lessons to ensure enrichment opportunities.		
Provided opportunities for students to generate essential questions.		
Used a variety of resources.		
Provided opportunities for students to reflect upon their work.		
Provided students opportunities to demonstrate their skills in formats conducive to their individual learning/presentation style.		
Provided opportunities to collect, share, reflect upon, and employ data to make corrections and adjustments.		
Used closure activities that tie this learning to the next unit.		

everything, let's examine the story of the two parents from Long Island, New York, who were frustrated by their son's lack of achievement in mathematics. The story serves as an excellent example of people not understanding what the schools expect of them or what they should expect of the schools. The father, a nuclear engineer, and the mother, a successful businesswoman, were meeting growing resistance from their son who was overwhelmed by the quantity of homework he was receiving. At first, he tried to keep up with the volume, but then he became increasingly frustrated by his inability to complete all of the assignments.

Time and time again, he really tried to do the work, but unfortunately he just didn't understand certain concepts. His teacher, however, just kept grading the homework he turned in, marked him low on problems he didn't solve, and then moved on with the in-class lessons. Fearing he was the only one unable to grasp and to apply what material was covered, the boy just shut down his efforts and, instead, devoted his energies into rationalizing his position and failure.

Not knowing what else to do, the parents tried to help him with the homework problems, but the son's entrenchment into failure prevented them from lifting him out of depression. And, since both of the parents were mathematical wizards who couldn't understand how their genes could fail to produce a math prodigy, they were easily frustrated with their own efforts to explain the concepts that were required to solve simple problems. Their intelligence got in the way of their effort to help. They concentrated on today's homework without seeing that the boy's overall base of understanding was weak. So despite the fact that the boy was getting answers on the homework, he didn't understand any better in class the next day. His inability to deal with the math homework then gave him an excuse for not doing homework in other subject areas as well. Frustration led to failure because his parents didn't know or understand what their role was in his educational process. They took him out of the public school system and placed him in a private school, where his frustration continues and will until the parents get involved the correct way.

How does this tie into unit design? The parents were looking at daily progress without understanding the final goal. Today's homework became paramount, but they didn't understand the big picture, how the problems tied in to the standards the boy was supposed to be learning. Had they requested a unit design from the teacher or had the teacher sent them one at the beginning, they probably would have had a clearer idea of where the boy was and where he was supposed to be going. They could have addressed the specifics easier and earlier had they known the goal. They would have been able to ask the necessary questions of the teacher. Unit design gives parents the broad picture so they can see where the individual pieces fit.

WHAT DID YOU DO IN SCHOOL TODAY?

Does this line sound familiar? Did you ever take a quiz or test, fail the results, and then hear your teacher say, "Now, we have to move on." Since you obviously didn't have the information down solid yet, how were you ever supposed to understand it now that the class was moving into phase two? Compounding failure is easy; it has happened to everyone. But, when parents see it happening to their own children, they have a tendency to lash out either at the child or the teacher. They normally accuse their child of the following: "You're not trying." "You aren't applying yourself." "You don't listen in class." "You don't ask enough questions." With the teacher, parents always say that Jimmy was a good student before he got in this class, but "You're going too fast."

A major part of the problem is that parents don't really know what to ask and what to expect of their children or their schools. "How did you do in school today?" or "What did you do in school today?" are not questions children can readily answer unless they are in a classroom where the standards to be covered for that day are posted and discussed, where goals are clear, where performance objectives are understood, where exemplars and rubrics are available so that students can assess their ongoing performance and make adjustments, and where teachers have set forth an environment for success. Another part of the problem is that parents often pick a minor issue without really seeing the crux of the problem. Their hit-or-miss approach doesn't address the needs of the student or of the teacher. "I don't know how to do that stuff" is not an excuse that parents should use in helping students. With parent and student working and learning together even on specific assignments, an educational bond can be established.

Unit design is a tool that teachers can use to help the students understand the goals, as well as to help the parents to comprehend how daily lessons and assignments are related to the overall picture. Knowing the overall expectations helps the parents to address problems more quickly and also assists them in asking relevant questions of both the teacher and the student. Communication lines become clearer, and the "But Jimmy didn't tell me you were doing that" starts to disappear. Likewise, parents can recognize where their own knowledge limitations need help, so they can make wiser recommendations on where and how their student gets the extra help necessary to succeed.

With that in mind, Figure 7.7 contains a checklist for parents to assist them in working with the student and the teacher.

WHAT MOST PEOPLE NEED TO KNOW

- Teachers need collaboration time to coordinate instruction, share data, or compare teaching experiences so they can adjust their methods of delivery. They need time to develop units, as well as single lessons. Administrators may arrange blocks of meeting time through the following:
  o Department meetings
  o Coverage by substitutes
  o After or before school meetings
  o Creative scheduling

- Professional development is necessary for teachers to become clearly informed of methods to design units, assess performance, gather data, and use the data to change and adjust.

- Teachers need opportunities to observe peers so they can learn from and support colleagues. and administrators need to provide the following:
  o Mentoring
  o Guidance
  o Easy access to data

- Teacher accountability is foremost in establishing and maintaining a standards-based educational system, and administrators need to provide the following:
  o Observation
  o Immediate feedback (to assist teachers in adjusting and implementing standards-based education)

Figure 7.7   Parent Checklist

PARENT CHECKLIST	YES	NO
I have obtained a complete set of the standards my child will be covering throughout this academic year.		
I have examined the student and parent unit plan and clearly understand both the components of the plan and my role in implementing it.		
I have asked my child what goals the teacher set for the class today.		
I have asked my child what help he or she needs to practice the skills learned today.		
I have asked my child to demonstrate what he or she has learned in school.		
I have looked at my child's schoolwork and have asked for explanations of some of his or her choices or understandings without criticizing them.		
I have asked my child to apply the day's learning in real-life situations at home (measuring chocolate syrup for milk, creating a time schedule, helping me to measure the length of material, writing a thank-you note, etc.) so that I can help the student to make connections between knowledge and application.		
I have tried to show my child that what he or she learned today was important.		
I have provided encouragement to my child to help work through errors.		
I have provided models and exemplars for my child to use as assessment pieces.		
I have set up a process to communicate with the teacher in order to get updates on the student's progress or problem areas, especially involving motivation, understanding, and application of knowledge.		
I have communicated to the teacher any difficulties my child has in interpreting, understanding, and completing the homework.		
I have helped my child to assess his or her performance by using the rubrics and assessment tools associated with the lesson.		
I have provided an appropriate place in my home where my child can complete work without interruption and can have time and space to reflect.		
I have provided the supplies and resources (pens, calculators, calendars, maps, etc.) necessary for my child to complete the work.		
I have provided encouragement for my child to use data to make corrections and adjustments.		
I have helped to provide scaffolding (steps) to assist my child to complete a goal successfully.		
I haven't used one of the following excuses: I'm too busy to help you, The schools are supposed to do that, This stuff is all different now and I can't help you, We didn't have this when I was a kid. . . .		

WHAT SOME PEOPLE NEED TO KNOW

Unit design is not an individual assignment but rather is a grade-level task. All teachers need to cover set standards using core materials. Enrichment should be built in for those students who can grasp and apply the standards with ease. Less is more, but only as long as there is consistency among teachers in covering the standards. This consistency must be monitored and supported.

- Administrators must make sure teachers have time to work in grade-level teams to coordinate and update units and assessments.

- Teacher-parent communication needs to be monitored to ensure that parents receive adequate information to become participants and not just observers in the process. Standardized forms should be made available to the teachers to use and fill out for the parents in order to allow this communication process to proceed smoothly.

- Teachers should have access to school or to individual Web sites in order to post lessons, provide support to students, or to communicate with parents.

SUMMARY

The following points sum up the gist of this chapter in that they stress the need for setting clear expectations, using assessments, controlling time effectively, and communicating results. They show that the focus of education is on what the learner knows and can do.

- The teacher, parent, and student are all part of a team in which clear expectations are presented up front, and methods of application of knowledge are varied to accommodate different learning styles.

- Unit design helps to focus learning for both the teacher and the student. It provides parents with an opportunity to get the overall picture and to ask relevant questions.

- Teachers must control time in order to complete coverage of the standards, collaborate on assessment design, allow students to reflect on their work, and to share successes with colleagues. They also need time to work on unit design.

- Communication between teacher and parent is a fundamental necessity to make any learning situation work to its maximum effectiveness.

Lesson Design 8

In the Robin Hood legend, Robin, disguised as a tinker, has to compete against the sheriff's handpicked man. When the other bowman hits the center of the target, the enthusiasm is taken out of the crowd as they see that no one can top that shot. Up steps Robin. He notches the arrow, sights the target, and unleashes his feathered projectile only to have it split his opponent's shaft. Robin has hit the middle of the middle, and the crowd explodes in joy. Even Robin, though he has revealed himself through his prowess and will be captured, is elated that he has demonstrated his expertise for all to see. Designing a lesson that fits into a unit that is standards-based is much like splitting an arrow in the center of a target. This is a moment when the teacher has demonstrated enough prowess to integrate content with method in order to produce a highly desirable outcome. While Robin's shot is probably looked at as one-in-a-million, teachers have to perform this feat multiple times daily; they have to hit a bull's-eye in designing a lesson so that their students truly learn and can apply the skills. The purpose of this section is to show how an educator can set such lofty goals and still always succeed.

HEY, I JUST FOLLOW THE CURRICULUM

Some teachers have all too often made one of the following statements:

- "I never really plan my lessons; they just come to me when I'm on my way to work. A lot of times the best lesson pops into my head just as I'm entering the classroom."

- "I've been teaching so long that I don't need to plan. I've done this all before."

- "I just follow the curriculum."

- "I was watching a program on television and I thought the kids might want to learn about that."

Unfortunately, none of these statements fit in with sound teaching practices, never mind with standards-based ones. Instead, at best, these concepts produce a haphazard approach to teaching that leaves the burden on the students to try to make sense out of the information they are being given. The result is that they often struggle in their attempts to tie the disjointed material into what they have been previously covering, never truly realizing what is relevant and what is relative. In short, the brain becomes confused in trying to form patterns. This often leads the students to ask the teacher to "tell us what you want us to do." Yet, their confusion isn't because they are unwilling to cooperate or participate, but rather because they don't know what the teacher expects of them. "Tell the students what you want them to do and you can expect that most students will do it" should be a teacher's philosophy.

QUESTIONS TO ASK

When a teacher has designed a unit to establish a scope and sequence to teach the standards, the most critical pieces of that unit are the individual lessons. They are integral to ensuring that not only has the bull's-eye been hit but that it has been mastered, and teachers can know that students have truly learned the material and can use it in real-world applications.

Before teachers begin to design a lesson, they must ask themselves the following questions:

- What should a student know and be able to do as a result of this lesson? How are the objectives of the lesson relevant to the standards that have been established?
- How will students demonstrate what they have learned? In short, how will the students be assessed and what form will that assessment take?
- How will the teacher find out what previous knowledge, skills, and experiences the students have had that they can apply to the present learning?
- How will the teacher assist the students to process the information and find patterns so they can make meaning from the new learning?
- How will the teacher check for understanding in an ongoing manner so appropriate strategies can be employed in a timely way?
- How can the teacher differentiate the lesson so that all students are positively engaged and working productively at their own pace?
- How will the teacher frame the lesson so students clearly understand the objectives, the reasons why learning the information is important, the directions, the procedures, and the assessment criteria?
- How will the teacher make the lesson meaningful by building in problem-solving and real-world applications?
- How will the teacher control the use of space to maximize student interaction and productivity?

WHERE THERE'S A NEED, THERE'S A WAY

Students have to have a reason to start the learning process each day and in each lesson. Bloom's Taxonomy starts with *knowledge* as the first rung on the six-step ladder; however, without a *need* to learn, the teacher often cannot engage the student's interest to acquire *knowledge*. Teachers, therefore, have to explain not only *what* a student should know but also *why* this knowledge is important beyond just for passing the next test or quiz. Since identifying purpose for a lesson not only ignites the student but sometimes relights the flame of learning in the teacher as well, this is the area that all teachers should address. Teachers need to have their intellectual candles rewicked often enough so they, too, understand the importance of the information they are presenting and the skills they are teaching. Ideally, as students learn something, they then have the opportunity to apply that knowledge or skill as soon and as often as possible in meaningful situations. In this way they see the value of the knowledge and skills they are acquiring. Although this is not always possible, teachers must constantly reinforce the *need* to know so that students actively pursue positive ends.

WHAT EVERYONE NEEDS TO KNOW

Before beginning to teach, a teacher has to have a clear idea of what constitutes a good, solid, standards-based lesson. Knowing all of the characteristics is meaningless unless a teacher can picture what all of the components look like together in application. A successful lesson looks like the following:

- At the beginning of the lesson, students are informed about what standard(s) they will be learning.

- The standard is posted where the students can see it and refer to it.

- The standard is written in a language the students can understand.

- Students are told why the standard is important to learn, as well as how the standard ties into the world inside and outside of the classroom. The teacher also discusses the standard with the students to make sure everyone has the same understanding.

- The students are given a clear objective for the lesson and should be shown how the objective ties into the standard.

- Students are provided with a method to assess their work (a rubric, model, whatever) and the scoring system is explained, or the teacher assists students in creating their own assessment device. In either case, the teacher covers all of the component parts, constantly checking for understanding, so students can see and judge how their end product should look.

- The lesson is related to the previous learning and experiences, and the teacher uses various techniques to see how much the students already know about the content.

- A variety of strategies are employed to get the students involved, making sure that the use of space and time are conducive to the instruction.

- The teacher checks for understanding frequently, and in various ways, throughout the lesson and adjusts the instruction accordingly for students.

Asking students if they "got it" or "have any questions" is not a complete way to check for understanding.

- Meaningful real-world application experiences are provided so that students may practice the skills both inside and outside of the classroom.

- The teacher provides closure to the lesson, and also ties it into the next day's learning.

- Homework assignments are provided only when they are meaningful and when they allow the students to practice the skills they have learned. Homework should not be thought of as busywork, a way to rationalize grades in a grade book, or a strategy to absorb part of a teaching period. It's not a place to introduce new material, a punishment for inattention in class, or an instrument to placate parents or administrators.

LESSON DESIGN STEPS

The teacher must undertake certain basic steps to ensure that the standards-based lesson is complete and addresses the learner's needs.

- Identify the performance objective upon which the students will be working.
- Identify what knowledge and skills are essential for:
  - Every student to know
  - Most students to know
  - Some students to know
- Identify the background knowledge the students need to bring in order to practice and to master the skills necessary to achieve the standard.
- Identify models or exemplars needed to assist the students to demonstrate that they understand the big idea and have the essential skills.
- Identify differentiating lessons and scaffolding steps to assist students who are having difficulty.
- Identify ways to frame the learning (communicate the standard, the objective, the lesson requirement, and the assessment):
  - Explain clearly what the students need to know and what they will be expected to do.
  - Relate the standard to real-life situations (*need*).
  - List and explain the assessments the student will need to know to perform the objective.
  - Explain how students will demonstrate what they have learned.
  - Provide models and exemplars that the students may use to provide them with an ongoing assessment.
  - Provide an agenda or an outline for the day.
  - Offer ways to check for understanding.
  - Provide ways for the students to summarize what they have learned, as well as reflection time for students to process the information.
  - Tie in what's learned to other areas of study and to problems outside of the classroom.

- Identify ways to know where the student is performing at the beginning of each unit (pretest, portfolio, conference, and the like).

- Identify ways to assist students in using prior knowledge and skills.

- Identify classroom activities that will help both the teacher and the students to assess progress toward mastery.

- Identify ways to utilize the physical dimensions of the classroom to maximize learning.

THE TRANSFER AND RETENTION OF LEARNING

In constructing learning activities for the students, the teacher should be aware of the transfer and retention rate of learning in the classroom as shown in Figure 8.1. This is a valuable tool because it allows teachers to structure lessons so that they have the greatest learning impact on the students.

While the lecture method is the safest choice for teachers because they are in total control of the information being presented, it's also the least effective for the students' learning. Many teachers encourage students to spend part of a period or part of a day in silent reading; the retention and transfer rate of learning is dramatically less than if the students read less but spend time in active group discussion about the reading. Watching a film or slide show in isolation without follow-up discussion or practice of the skills learned produces an almost insignificant amount of retention and transfer. The teacher should remember that if

Figure 8.1   Transfer and Retention

Learning Activity	Retention, Transfer, and Application of Learning in the Classroom
Lecture	Least amount of retention since students act in a passive manner and aren't personally engaged in applying the learning. Emphasis is on teacher teaching and not on learner learning.
Reading	Retention is still low since the student doesn't have the opportunity to share ideas and observations, nor the means to apply the learning.
Audio-Visual	Still a passive activity not involving application; does increase retention slightly in that it engages multiple senses.
Demonstration	Higher retention, but only if the student is actively engaged in the demonstration by physically participating.
Discussion Group	Interaction with peers requires the student to test ideas and to be able to defend conclusions, making future application easier.
Practice "Real-World" Application	High retention and transfer since students are using assessment to refine the final, meaningful product.
Teach Others/Immediate Use of Learning	Highest retention, since students have already assessed, made changes and corrections, and are applying the learning.

SOURCE: Adapted from the learning pyramid developed by Edgar Dale (1969).

teaching is performed correctly, the instructor is creating a cadre of "student teachers" who not only assist in developing understanding in their peers but also reinforce understanding and application in themselves.

The teacher should also address the following additional considerations in lesson design:

- While rows of desks provide easy attendance taking, they are not always the best method for teacher accessibility to students.
  - *Small groups/cooperative learning.* Tables or clusters of desks and chairs
  - *Class discussion.* Circle or square or horseshoe with teacher in the center
  - *Overall best.* Horseshoe or double horseshoe with students facing each other

- A teacher controls time on learning.
  - The teacher should pause three to five seconds after asking a question to allow students time to process the information (Stahl, 1994).
  - The teacher should pause three to five seconds after the student gives an answer in order to allow students the time to process the information (Stahl, 1994).

- Allow movement during an activity, at least every 37 minutes—more often for younger students.

- Break new skills and information into small chunks and should provide short practices as soon as possible.

- Students should be moved to real-life applications as quickly as conditions permit.

- With complex concepts, a slower pace and more immediate practices help students grasp each of the component pieces as well as the whole.

- The entire school is a resource. Halls, gyms, auditoriums, fields, and cafeterias can be used as spaces to practice measurement, conduct debates, carry out experiments, lay out large projects, display work, conduct surveys, gather data, and practice presentations.

- The teacher should observe peer teachers using time, space, movement, and pacing in their own classrooms. To reiterate, administrators must be proactive in using resources to find or make time for teachers to do this crucial exercise. Modeling is an excellent presentation tool. Peer observation is a less stressful method of learning. Watching a peer teacher structure and present a lesson helps an individual educator to design his or her lesson more efficiently and effectively.

- The skill level of the class must be analyzed before the lesson begins, and potential problems that the lesson could create for specific students should be uncovered and possible solutions addressed.

LESSON DESIGN PLANNER

The lesson design planner in Figure 8.2 is similar to the unit design template (see Figure 7.1) in that it focuses on an outline format. There is more specificity

Figure 8.2 Lesson Design Planner

LESSON DESIGN PLANNER	DATE:

TEXT(S):

LESSON OBJECTIVE (GOAL):

STANDARDS:	REASONS WHY STANDARD IS IMPORTANT TO LEARN:
ESSENTIAL QUESTIONS:	METHOD(S) OF ASSESSMENT:
SPECIFIC VOCABULARY:	MATERIALS/TECHNOLOGY REQUIRED:
ACTIVITIES:	TIME ALLOTMENT:
SCAFFOLDING REQUIRED:	DIFFERENTIATION:
REAL-WORLD APPLICATION:	HOMEWORK:

in that the teacher is usually working with a single standard and must show its relevance to the big picture. Framing the lesson is a crucial part of the process. Students need to know why the standard is important, as well as how and where the skills may be applied in the real world. While the teacher knows the answer to these questions, he or she must not assume that students also know the reasons. If possible, planning a real-world application that students can use as immediately as possible reinforces the learning tremendously. Students then can teach others (see Figure 8.1) and maximize retention.

The lesson analysis template for teachers (see Figure 8.3) is an aid to identify potential problems and possible solutions before they arise in the classroom.

The lesson design rubric for teacher self-assessment (see Figure 8.4) provides a way for teachers to assess their own performance in lesson design.

Teachers experiencing major difficulty should have an immediate opportunity to discuss the problem with colleagues or administrators (team leaders, department chairs, coordinators) and to be provided with possible, workable

Figure 8.3 Lesson Analysis Guide

1. What is the goal of the lesson? What will the student have to learn?

2. What are the skills or what is the knowledge necessary to complete the assignment or task?

3. What strategies can be used to prevent problems that would hinder the student from completing the task or assignment?

Student Name	Potential Problem	Possible Solution

Figure 8.4   Rubric for Self-Assessment

CHECK BOX	Excellent = 4	Proficient = 3	Average = 2	Not Yet =1
CATEGORIES	*4*	*3*	*2*	*1*
Performance Objective	Clear	Appropriate	Adequate	Out of sequence
Essential Learning	Includes all students	Includes many students	Includes some students	Irrelevant
Skill Analysis	Material is important to know.	Material has some relevance.	Material is mainly nice to know.	Trivial
Rubric or Performance Task	Clear to all students	Clear to most students	Vague	Unclear
Models or Exemplars	Precise	Good	Ambiguous or difficult to understand	Poor
Differentiated Lessons	Provided for all contingencies	Provided for most situations	Insufficient	Missing
Framing the Learning	Clear, precise for all students	Clear for most students	Clear for some students	Unclear
Student Knowledge Base	Teacher knows what most students bring to the lesson.	Teacher knows what some students bring to the lesson.	Teacher is unclear about what most students bring.	Teacher is unaware of the student's knowledge base.
Active Learning Experience	Lesson allows all students to apply the learning.	Lesson allows some application.	Lesson allows little application.	Lesson allows no application.
Relevance	Assignments, projects, and homework help all students to see the relevance of the lesson.	Assignments help most students to see the relevance of the lesson.	Assignments help some students to see the relevance of the lesson.	Few students see relevance of lesson.
Classroom Activities	Relevant with clear focus and multiple assessment strategies	Relevant with clear focus and some assessment strategies	Few planned assessment strategies	Poor
Learning Environment	Maximizes instruction, allows for differentiated lessons with minor restructuring.	Promotes instruction, allows for multiple types of lessons.	Adequate	Poor
Use of Data to Drive Instruction	Uses multiple and ongoing data sources to monitor learning.	Uses some data sources to monitor learning.	Uses few data sources to monitor learning.	Uses no data sources.

TOTAL POINTS	*SCALE*	*CONCERNS*	*STRATEGIES*
	45–52 Excellent 37–44 Proficient 29–36 Average 13–28 Weak		

solutions. The teacher should be provided with methods and time for other than just tests or quizzes to determine a student's prior knowledge or skill level. Oral response sessions, student conferences, demonstrations, summaries, and so on, are closer to real-world assessments. Test questions aren't always phrased correctly and often lend themselves to individual interpretation.

WHAT MOST PEOPLE NEED TO KNOW

Middle managers play a vital role in providing feedback to the teachers, assisting them in meeting collegially, securing materials and forms, and acting as a liaison with the administration around the key issue of time.

Lesson plan books should be kept up-to-date and should be checked once every two weeks by an administrator. Helpful comments, including praise, should be made in the text and then the plans should be returned in a timely fashion. Teachers experiencing difficulty should have an immediate opportunity to discuss the problem and to be provided with administrative support to assist in the creation of possible, workable solutions.

WHAT SOME PEOPLE NEED TO KNOW

Although designing a lesson appears to be removed from the day-to-day considerations of an administrator, the converse is true. The daily lessons are precisely what constitute the learning chain, and their importance can't be understated. All of the efforts of the top administration should be to ensure that these lessons are taught in a standards-based method by teachers who are dedicated to the principle that schools operate for students to learn and to apply their knowledge. The task of the administrator is to provide ways to make that lesson progress without external obstacles. In that regard, the administrator should know the following:

- Blocks of time must be built into the schedule (and often negotiated with unions) to allow teachers in grade level groups or departments to meet and to discuss issues and solutions. Districts may buy time (compensate teachers for additional time in the work day), restructure certain days in the week to create time blocks for teacher use, structure professional development time more creatively, or use already required before or after school time more efficiently.

- All lessons taken from the Internet should be conformed to the format established in the district. Administrators need to create a "unit and lesson plan architecture" to provide consistency in the way these items are created and used throughout the district.

SUMMARY

In creating a successful standards-based lesson, teachers must be constantly aware of the following questions:

- What should a student know and be able to do as a result of this lesson?
- How will the students be assessed and what form will that assessment take?
- How will the teacher find out what students already know that they can apply to the present learning?
- How can students be helped to find patterns so that they can make meaning from the new learning?
- How will the teacher check for understanding in an ongoing manner?
- How can the lesson be differentiated so that all students are positively engaged and working productively at their own pace?
- How can the lesson be framed so that students clearly understand the objectives, the reasons why learning the information is important, the directions, the procedures, and the assessment criteria?
- How can building in problem-solving and real-world applications make the lesson more meaningful?
- How can space be used to maximize student interaction and productivity?

9 Differentiation

"One size fits all" is a descriptor many people see when thumbing through various clothing catalogs. Yet, in a recent interview on a television style show, a fashion consultant said that people need to try on commercially made clothing before they purchase the items to make sure that garments fit properly. She even said that women's jeans labeled with the same size could vary greatly in fit. In light of that, certain Internet sites are offering custom-made clothing at wholesale prices. The customer takes a variety of measurements (not just the waist and length type, but also calf, thigh, hips, abdomen, and so on) and a computer designs a custom-fit garment exclusively for that individual. Clever idea or just common sense? How come nobody ever thought of this before? Well, they did, but mass production just seems easier, and people learn to live with too loose or too snug. The people in the know, however, have always had their clothes custom made.

How does any of this relate to education? For many years, a "one size fits all" has been the norm. The one-room schoolhouse is a perfect example of this mentality. Even in the early 1990s, the theory was that if a teacher could teach one child, that teacher could teach 35 children. The premise was based more on budgetary data than on educational data, but many schools subscribed to the idea and increased class size. Teachers reacted by saying "I can't do this," so class sizes were cut, but then school districts started to demand individualization for students. Now teachers were expected to create individualized lesson plans for 25 different students on a daily basis. Once again, teachers said, "I can't do this." With conflicting demands upon them, many of the teachers retreated to a holding pattern, to the old lecture format where teachers "taught" and students "listened." After all, that pattern was considered safe since many educators had come from systems where those tactics had been used on them. Although they hadn't liked it then, they understood the steps and fell into a comfort zone. Plus, this teacher-controlled lecture format was a lot easier since it occupied the students' time thereby making classroom management supposedly easier.

In a nearby school district, the administrators decided to implement a rotating long-block schedule where a different period would be doubled each day and another period would be dropped. The idea was that teachers could use the second half of the double block to provide guided practice for the students and could address individual learning issues. Instead, the vast majority of the teachers used the second part to continue to lecture to the students. They felt they had better control over the students when they stood in front of the class and kept the students "occupied." Other teachers scheduled movies to fill these double blocks. The bottom line was that the majority of teachers wanted to "teach" rather than focus on having students learn.

TEACHING VERSUS LEARNING

Recently, a more vocal debate has opened up on teaching versus learning. Is the role of the teacher in the classroom to present enough facts and data to increase the core knowledge base so that some of it sticks on everyone in range, or is it to create student learners who possess understanding of the material, can make connections, and can apply what they have learned? In the book *The Child Buyer*, by John Hersey, the guidance director, Mr. Cleary, sums up his view of the protagonist's teacher by saying, "Her pedagogical methodology is unorthodox. Her techniques of encouraging wholesome motivation for mastery of critical skills, habits, understandings, knowledge, and attitudes, and of achieving dynamic personality of the whole child to both the learning situation and the life situation are, though soundly rooted in the developmental tradition, rather eccentric, and indeed they defy exact characterization." The state senator then asks, "But can she teach, Mr. Cleary?" To which Cleary responds, "The children won't tell us" (Hersey, 1960, p. 39). This attitude that a teacher is teaching whether or not students are learning still pervades classrooms across the country.

Look at punctuation for an example. Most students have been drilled on when to use certain forms of punctuation, but relatively few understand why punctuation is necessary. Use a comma after an introductory adverbial clause and a semicolon to separate two independent clauses that are not joined by a coordinating conjunction, unless the independent clauses are short, are two rules one memorizes, but why does a person use these two forms of punctuation to the exclusion of other forms or of each other? If someone would have told the students the *why* in the first place, they could have figured out the *when* on their own. However, teaching the when is easier because everyone has to memorize the rule at the same time and use the same examples or fill in the same sentences or do the same exercises. There is no differentiation. That leads to the focus of this chapter.

[handwritten note: Teach the "Why?" Not the "When?"]

DIFFERENTIATION DEFINED

[handwritten note: Montessori Materials]

Basically defined, differentiation is a method to create a variety of strategies so that students of different interests, abilities, readiness, or backgrounds experience effective paths to learn, understand, connect with, and use their knowledge. There are different ways for all students in the same class to look at curriculum content, process information, make connections to previous learning, and deliver what they have learned in an assortment of presentation styles. Differentiation provides them with the opportunity to use time in learning to

[handwritten note: How going to learn concept? Like special education for everyone.]

develop proficiency and mastery in skills necessary to move on to the next level. Similarly, it allows teachers to focus on student learning as an integral part of the teaching process and not just as a by-product.

Differentiation is not "extra." It's not having students do extra assignments, answer extra questions, write extra compositions, or conduct extra experiments if this is based on what students already know and can do. Think about shoveling snow off your driveway. If you can do it in an hour without exerting yourself to an uncomfortable or health-threatening degree, why would you listen to someone tell you to slow down and do it in two hours? What if that person said that now that you have shoveled the driveway, you have to shovel the backyard for more experience? Shoveling is not a highly structured skill that needs extended practice or application, and shoveling the backyard really accomplishes no additional meaningful purpose. This is the old "extra credit" myth. Basically, the student is saying, "I can already do this but I want more points, so can I do it again for you?" Or the teacher is saying, "The first time I tested you, you weren't ready, but I tested you anyway. Now I see you are ready, so I will give you and me another chance. Only, let's not admit I was wrong the first time, and now I'll make it up to you by calling this grade *extra credit*. Even though this activity is meaningless, we both agree to play the game." Differentiation is not meant to be punitive; instead, it's a tool to allow students to take more ownership of their learning.

LEARNING STYLES VERSUS TEACHING STYLES

Recent studies have indicated the following statistics regarding how individuals process information (Montgomery, 1995):

- 67% of learners are *active processors.* They learn best by doing something physical with the information, such as conducting an experiment or drawing a picture. *yes*

- 32% of learners are *reflective processors.* They operate best by processing in their heads, such as thinking through a series of topics before putting anything down on paper. *yes*

- 57% of learners are *sensing processors.* They prefer data and facts; they like making lists and focus on the *what* of any situation. In literature, they would like a chronological plot.

- 42% of learners are *intuitive processors.* They prefer theories or interpretations of facts and data; they focus on the *why* of any situation.

- 69% of learners are *visual processors.* They prefer charts, maps, diagrams, graphs, and pictures. *yes!*

- 30% of learners are *verbal processors.* They prefer the spoken or written word.

- 71% of learners are *sequential processors.* They prefer to make connections between individual steps.

big picture first

- 28% of learners are *global processors.* They have to get the overall picture before they can begin to see where the pieces fit. They need to see the cover picture on a jigsaw puzzle box before they can even think about linking the pieces. *yes*

Look at a typical classroom and see how these percentages now have individual faces. Differentiation is necessary to provide growth and success for each of these students.

In a college amphitheater, a student sat among 199 peers listening to a lecture on quantitative analysis. Three times a week for 50 minutes per session for 14 weeks, the student took copious notes and transcribed everything the lecturer wrote on the board. The student rarely understood most of what the lecturer was saying but filled notebook after notebook with seemingly important information. A fellow student sitting in the next seat wrote down nothing and proceeded to knit an afghan during the lectures. At the end of the course, the first student took the final exam and passed the course with a C. The fellow student got a B and ended up with an afghan as well. The first student was an active processor with a visual bent. Lecture didn't suit this student's learning style. The fellow student was a reflective processor with a verbal bent. Lecture was exactly what this student needed. The lecturer, however, did not differentiate among all of the students, so some fell into "just getting by" while others flourished because their needs were being met.

WHAT EVERYONE NEEDS TO KNOW

Teachers must realize that no two students are alike, nor do they learn in identical ways. This fact, however, should not frighten the teacher into thinking that he or she has to prepare a separate lesson plan for every student that appears in that classroom through the course of the day. With skillful use of differentiation, students of mixed abilities can grow together at their own rates.

- Even though students have different learning styles, the basic skills and content can remain standard.

- The focus is not on teachers teaching, but on students learning.

- Teachers need not differentiate a lesson into the same number of ways as there are students in the classroom.

- All differentiation starts with assessing students to determine where they are in relationship to knowledge base, nearness to meeting the standards, and readiness to go on.

- Before differentiation begins, students and parents must be informed about the expectations for students so the "fairness" issue is resolved.
  - Students and parents must receive a copy of the grade-level expectations for each subject area.
  - They must be made aware of different learning styles and methods of presentation.

- They must be informed that all student expectations are the same, but the ways to achieve these goals may require some students to work at different tasks at different times than their peers.

- Differentiation can be used in the classroom in the following ways (Theroux, 2004):
  - *Differentiating the content.* Students can work faster or slower on the content either by getting additional teacher help or skipping the parts they already know and dealing with more complex problem-solving situations.
  - *Differentiating the learning activities.* Students tackle the key ideas or standards through tasks of varying difficulty, all coordinated to bring them to the same goals as the other students.
  - *Differentiating the product.* Student presentation is more-or-less exacting, depending on the level of mastery of the standards.
  - *Differentiating the environment.* Student learning styles differ, and the teacher must make accommodations to allow students access to an environment conducive to their needs. This may require more use of visuals, different types of student grouping, peer work or conferencing, a reflective time, a hands-on area, and so on.

- Ongoing assessment is built into the curriculum so teachers know the readiness and the ability of the students to move on.

- Teachers approach the lessons with definite strategies (see Figure 9.1) that can accommodate groups of learners.

- The students should be encouraged to create products that emphasize their strengths and demonstrate their learning styles.

- Teachers can also differentiate instruction through the use of the following:
  - Supplemental texts/materials
  - Creation of learning areas within the classroom
  - Independent research projects
  - Flexible seating
  - Varying graphic organizers
  - Alternative assessments

- The students should have the opportunity to create meaningful products that have application to real-world settings.

- Teachers must be flexible and adjust their predominant teaching style to accommodate the individual learning styles of the students. For the majority of learners, a straight teacher-lecture style is the least effective method of ensuring learning. Current research suggests that more students are generally active, sensing, visual, sequential learners.

Assign a project in any classroom. Tell the students that they each have to write a 500-word paper on the topic to address specifics that you list on the board. Watch most of them sit passively by, trying to cope. Instead, assign a topic and show flexibility in how the project results can be presented. Let students loose to form their own groups and decide on a mode of presentation. Immediately, the following events occur:

Figure 9.1   Strategies for Accommodating Groups of Learners

Adjusting the Questions	During large group discussions, the teacher elicits questions about the subject from the students. Then, the teacher classifies the questions into categories of difficulty and assigns small groups to address the answers, making sure that students with greater needs are in one group, those with average needs are in another, and exceptional learners are in the third. The major questions are doled out accordingly. As one group finishes, the members create a method of presentation and deliver it to the remaining groups.
	Alternative Method: Each student creates a question around a topic or problem. The questions are collected and read aloud. The class votes on which three questions are to be considered for examination. After the three questions are selected, copies of the three questions are made and distributed to the students. The remaining questions are posted on walls, the board, or elsewhere. Each student in the class will make a written, oral, or combination of both presentation on two questions. At least one, if not both of the questions, must come from the three-question list. The second question may come from the questions posted around the room. Students and the teacher create a rubric that addresses the quality of the content, proof, and so on, of the final product.
Student Pairs	Students select a topic from a list brainstormed by the class (topics relate to the standards being covered). Students are then paired up by the teacher according to level of readiness and ability to research the topic, create visual or aural aids, select a method of presentation, and devise a form of assessment to determine if they have learned and can apply the knowledge. The students, still in pairs, deliver their presentation to other pairs as the teacher monitors the activity, offering direct instruction where needed.
Step Lessons	The teacher begins by creating a performance objective for the lesson, complete with condition, task, criteria, all associated with a standard. To differentiate, the teacher changes the condition, the criteria, or both; but the task remains the same. In this way, students of different readiness or ability can proceed at their own pace through the steps, each step focusing on higher order thinking and application skills while reinforcing the standard. Successful completion of a step, based on a rubric, allows the student to proceed to the next level. The steps may be arranged in a progression of higher order thinking skills, with the first step focusing on acquiring knowledge, the second with an application phase, and the third in critical analysis. Students work at their own pace (with or without direct teacher involvement) and progress through the layers, building on previously mastered skills.

SOURCE: Adapted from "Differentiating Instruction" by Priscilla Theroux, 2004, available at http://members.shaw.ca/priscillatheroux/differentiation.htm.

- Most students scurry to find peers with whom they share a common interest.

- Most students quickly offer suggestions that reflect their learning style: "Let's get your father's video camera and create a skit." "I'll draw the picture and Peter can make the chart." "Why don't we make a newspaper that highlights some of Jay Gatsby's activities?" "Betty can write the playwright's biography, Janet can summarize the plot of the play, Judy and I will collect a bunch of critical reviews." "Now, make a topographical map of Ulysses' voyage. We'll need a 3-foot by 3-foot board, some clay, paints . . ."

- Student interests are activated and their grasp, their level of readiness, is enhanced (see Figure 9.2).

DIFFERENTIATED STEP LESSONS: METHOD 1

Lessons are differentiated in a number of ways; this section discusses two of them. They both accomplish the identical purpose and include the same steps but are worded slightly differently. Some teachers grasp the first method very easily while others gravitate toward the second; the end results are the same.

- *Start with the standard.* You must know where you are going and what it will look like when you get there. This is what you want the students to learn.

- *Create the assessment to the lesson.* Create assessments based on the steps. A single assessment piece may cover more than one step.

- *Identify the big picture, the general goal.* Usually the general goal can be expressed in one or two words (three at the most). Examples: fractions, spelling, weather, amendments, graphing, nutrition, decimals.

- *Identify the specific goal.* What do you want the students to know at the end of the lesson regardless of how quickly they progress through the steps? Example: Fractions are part of a whole; *i* before *e* except after *c*; there are both high and low pressure areas; amendments are additions to the Constitution; commas are used to separate items in a series; veto rights of the president.

- *Determine what you'll differentiate.* Differentiating the *content* (what you want students to learn). Differentiating the *learning activities* (the way they make sense out of the content). Differentiating the *products* (often a project). Differentiating the *environment* (the conditions under which they learn).

- *Determine how you'll differentiate.* *Readiness* is based on the ability levels of the students when beginning, *interest* is based on their curiosity of the subject matter, *profile* deals with the way students learn or present material. Pick one area that best serves the students in regard to this lesson.

- *Determine how many differentiated steps you'll need.* You may have two or three steps (just beginning, developing skills, proficiency to mastery, basic information, application knowledge, critical judgment). The steps build on each other. Use Bloom's Taxonomy to determine the higher order thinking skills that each step will address. When creating steps for gifted students, do them according to readiness.

SAMPLE STEP LESSONS USING METHOD 1

Standard: Fractions

General goal: Understanding fractions

Specific goal: Seeing how fractions represent part of the whole

Assessment: Students will explain how many equal parts there are and show how they know the parts are equal. They will compare the parts to exemplars.

Step 1: Using two paper circles to represent pizza and two squares to represent sandwiches, students, working in pairs, must show how to share the food equally with each person getting the exact same amount of pizza and sandwiches. They must then show how to share equally with 4 people; then with 8 people. They may fold and cut the paper.

Step 2: Using three paper circles (pizza) and three squares (sandwiches), students, working in groups of three, must show how to share the food equally with each person getting the exact same amount of pizza and sandwiches. They must then show how to share equally with 6 people, then 9 people, then 12 people. Then have the students start with a rectangle (a cake), and divide it equally into pieces for 3, 6, 9, and 12 people.

Step 3: Using paper rectangles (sandwiches) and triangles (pie slices), students, in pairs, determine how to share the food in three different ways to get equal parts. They must answer the following questions: Are there different ways to divide each shape equally? How many ways are there? Which shapes—circles, squares, rectangles, triangles—are easier to divide equally? Why?

Standard: Character

General goal: Understanding characters

Specific goal: Seeing how characters reveal themselves through what they say, what they do, and what others say about them

Assessment: Students will explain who the important characters are, tell two important things about each one to the teacher, and tell three things Cinderella does to show she is a good person. For layer 3, students will use a simple rubric to assess content and presentation.

Step 1: List all of the important characters in *Cinderella* and tell two important things about each one. When your work has been checked, move on to number 2.

Step 2: What are three important things that Cinderella does that show she is a good person? After your work has been checked, move on to number 3.

Step 3: Tell what happens to Cinderella, Prince Charming, the stepmother, and the stepsisters after the fairy tale ends. Describe what living "happily ever after" means.

Standard: Analyzing character

General goal: Character and theme

Specific goal: Seeing how the interaction of characters with their individual and group circumstances demonstrates their humanity

Assessment: Writing rubrics

Text: Lord of the Flies (Golding, 1954)

Step 1: In a paragraph, describe why Jack appears to become more savage than does Ralph. Use the rubric to assess your response. After your work has been checked, move on to number 2.

Step 2: Both Piggy and Simon help to reveal the true nature of Ralph. In three paragraphs, discuss what side of Ralph each character reveals and how these revelations are important to Ralph's relationship to Jack. Use the rubric to assess your response. After your work has been checked, move on to number 3.

Step 3: In a paper of at least five paragraphs, discuss the scene in which Simon confronts the Lord of the Flies and parallel this to the final scene of the novel where Ralph meets the naval officer on the beach. Tie the significance of the scenes to the theme of the novel.

DIFFERENTIATED STEP LESSONS: METHOD 2

To differentiate, the first thing to do is go to the performance objective that is based on the standard. Start with the task (what you want students to know and be able to do in relationship to the standard being covered). Now, create the condition and the criteria associated with the task. You have created the first step. All students must demonstrate proficiency at this step before moving on. Some students will be able to do so quickly, while others may need more teacher assistance or scaffolding. To create additional differentiated step lessons, do the following:

1. Keep the same task. In this way, students are exercising higher order thinking skills involving the same standard.

2. Change the condition, the criteria, or both, depending upon what skill level the students will be demonstrating at this next step.

3. Repeat this procedure for additional steps.

Think back to the original pyramid in Chapter 1. Differentiated step 1 is *what everyone needs to know*; step 2 is *what most people need to know*; step 3 is *what some people need to know.* Through differentiation, all of the students will be actively engaged in working on the same standard; each student will learn the basic skills necessary to perform that standard successfully; most students can apply those skills in more difficult problem-solving situations; and some students will completely master that standard.

SAMPLE STEP LESSONS USING METHOD 2

STEP 1

CONDITION: Using American pennies, . . .

TASK: . . . the student will be able to calculate how many pennies can fit in a rectangle in a single layer . . .

CRITERIA: . . . if the rectangle measures 4 inches by 6 inches, and with none of the pennies touching the boundary lines of the rectangle.

STEP 2

CONDITION: Using American pennies and dimes, . . .

TASK: . . . the student will be able to calculate exactly how many pennies can fit in a rectangle in a single layer . . .

CRITERIA: . . . if the rectangle measures 4 inches by 6 inches, and you also have to use four dimes, with none of the pennies or dimes touching the boundary lines of the rectangle.

STEP 3

CONDITION: Using American pennies, nickels, and dimes, . . .

TASK: . . . the student will be able to calculate exactly how many pennies can fit in a 4 inch by 6 inch rectangle in a single layer . . .

CRITERIA: . . . if you also have to use three dimes and three nickels, with none of the coins touching the boundary lines of the rectangle.

DIFFERENTIATED CLASSROOM 101

For a quick review, look at the basic requirements for differentiation:

- Differentiate based on readiness, interest, and profile.
- Differentiate at a pace that is comfortable for everyone, including the teacher.
- Deliver instructions carefully and clearly. Check for understanding often.
- Make sure students (and parents) understand the difference between *equal* and *fair*. All students are working on the same standard (*equal*) but at different levels of skill and application (*fair*).
- Make sure students have options for getting help when the teacher is busy with another student.
- Give students as much responsibility for their learning as possible.
- Make sure students understand group processes and the use of assessment devices.
- Use flexible grouping.
- Make sure each student's assignment is equally interesting, equally appealing, and equally focused on the main concept. All tasks must be perceived as worthwhile and valuable. No fluff, busywork, or time killers.
- Understand that not all students will get through all the steps, but every student must get through the first step.

- When differentiating based on readiness, the teacher may wish to consult the chart in Figure 9.2 to determine which verbs trigger the clearest responses in the learners.

The checklist in Figure 9.3 is a helpful tool that allows the teacher to see that the classroom environment is conducive to learning.

WHAT MOST PEOPLE NEED TO KNOW

In order for teachers to use differentiation strategies, middle managers must serve as mentors as well as advocates. They must establish a positive relationship with the teachers so that risk-taking for the purpose of growth is encouraged.

- Collaboration time is necessary for teachers to develop and to share strategies. This time must be made available by flexible scheduling; the use of aids or substitutes; in team, grade-level, department, and faculty meetings; or through negotiation. Time is the key for all standards-based progress.

- Administrative observers, either in walkthroughs or in formal evaluation, need to encourage teacher flexibility through the use of differentiation strategies.

- Administrators should understand that student-centered learning environments are part of the process of mastery of the standards. Students actively working together should be the norm rather than the exception. Administrators need to use the language of empowerment between teachers, as well as to encourage its use between teacher and student.

- Teachers must be provided with professional development training to determine student readiness, learning styles, and uses of motivational techniques.

WHAT SOME PEOPLE NEED TO KNOW

To maximize the time that the teacher has in unit and lesson design, the administrators need to provide all teachers with the tools and materials necessary for successful differentiation to take place. In that regard, teachers, middle managers, and administrators need to begin with a realistic needs survey that complements the requirements for differentiation in a standards-based classroom.

- Performance objectives, performance assessments, required and supplementary texts, and materials must be in place before differentiation can be used effectively. Time needs to be provided so that these tasks can be completed.

- Parents must be provided with a list of the following grade-level materials: subject standards, grade-level expectations, performance objectives,

Figure 9.2 Verbs Associated With Learning Styles

LEARNING STYLES	READINESS VERBS	ACTIVITIES
Active Processor	Design, illustrate, build, show, conduct, make, solve	Design a diorama . . . Illustrate a point . . . Build a model of . . . Show the reaction . . . Conduct an experiment . . . Make a flow timeline . . . Solve the puzzle . . .
Reflective Processor	Assess, justify, imagine, determine, interpret, rate	Assess the paper . . . Justify the verdict . . . Imagine the choices . . . Determine the number . . . Interpret the mood . . . Rate the performance . . .
Sensing Processor	List, outline, categorize, classify, identify, locate	List seven facts about . . . Outline the steps . . . Categorize the names . . . Classify the insects . . . Identify the types . . . Locate the capitols . . .
Intuitive Processor	Formulate, predict, relate, verify	Formulate an idea . . . Predict the events . . . Relate this to . . . Verify your opinion . . .
Visual Processor	Describe, list, name, show, draw, chart, point out, demonstrate	Describe the colors . . . List the nouns . . . Name the muscles . . . Show the features . . . Draw the picture . . . Chart the progress . . . Point out the details . . . Demonstrate the ways . . .
Verbal Processor	Discuss, explain, state, debate, argue, tell	Discuss the methods . . . Explain the theory . . . State the reason . . . Debate the issue . . . Argue the facts . . . Tell the class . . .
Sequential Processor	Link, connect, associate, join, unite	Link the character to . . . Connect the steps . . . Associate the events to . . . Join the tables into . . . Unite the features into . . .
Global Processor	See, understand, assume, recognize	See the whole . . . Understand the parts . . . Assume the unit is . . . Recognize the entire . . .

Figure 9.3   Classroom Environment Checklist

DIFFERENTIATED LEARNING ENVIRONMENT	YES	NO	POSSIBLE SOLUTIONS
Students are not always grouped alphabetically.			
Desks are not individually owned nor are students always bound to a specific space.			
Desks are arranged in patterns for productivity rather than just in rows.			
Students have access to supplementary materials that cover a broad range of readiness and ability.			
There are hands-on areas.			
The day's standards and goals are posted.			
Student products and ideas are reflected in the room.			
The room is a "safe" environment where students can share ideas with each other and the teacher and can take intellectual and creative risks.			
The class operates using clear guidelines based on student needs.			
The teacher shares the teaching with the students.			
Students are allowed to make choices to become independent learners.			
Students are actively engaged in the learning process.			
Students have a clear understanding of the performance objectives, as well as the assessment pieces.			
Students are asking and answering open-ended questions.			
Students are applying their learning in real-world problem-solving situations.			
Students understand that their peers may be engaged in other performance levels of the same standard.			
The teacher has provided sufficient time for the students to complete their learning successfully.			

performance assessments, and definitions of key terminology with examples.

- Differentiation has to be stressed across grade levels and throughout the district.

SUMMARY

Differentiation is crucial in the standards-based model, since it allows students to proceed at a constructive pace toward mastery. Teachers can differentiate the content, product, activities, or environment to produce positive results. Using readiness of the students, their interest, or their profile, teachers can create learning experiences that are geared to each student in the classroom. Because performance objectives and performance assessments are a key to the process, teachers can manipulate parts of each to create differentiated lessons. Students and parents must understand that having students working at different levels, even with different texts, on the same standards, does not violate "fairness" in the classroom.

10 Scaffolding

All too often scientists, mathematicians, celestial explorers, educators, and the like either create complex terms (quite often in Latin) to identify new objects and theories, or they redefine words that already have a common, easily understood meaning. These new definitions often run in contrast to the generally accepted perception creating, at best, confusion and, at worst, total chaos in a person's thought process. The reason is that the average person has no clear image related to the new word or phrase to connect it to previous learning. People's minds go in the direction of the pictures that they create. No mental picture is readily associated with terms such as *performance objective, differentiation*, or *multiple intelligences*, so the learner generally ends up memorizing a definition and examining numerous examples before the "I got it" phase sets in. Fortunately, the term *scaffolding* creates the exact picture the learner needs in order to make a connection with the desired meaning. A scaffold is a support structure that is used to assist in building something new or strengthening something old. After it's used to accomplish its purpose, the scaffolding is removed, and the structure, now deemed sound, stands on its own.

DEFINING SCAFFOLDING

A few years ago, the Statue of Liberty was encased in scaffolding as it was being repaired for its bicentennial. At the time, the scaffolding was essential to the construction crew that labored to firm up the statue and preserve the lady with the torch so she could sit in New York harbor in all her splendor. The renovation was completed successfully and the scaffolding was later removed. The support structure stands only as long as it is needed; it does not become a part of the finished product.

The same holds true in education; the real scaffold is the teacher assessing the student's present knowledge and providing proper support structures to get the student to the next level of learning. The scaffold helps to eliminate the problems or blocks that may arise within the student, such as an inability to make a connection to the new learning, a dislike of the material caused by a lack of success in application, or frustration that produces an "I give up" attitude. As the student progresses in utilizing the scaffolding, grasping the knowledge base, and applying it to new problem solving, the teacher reduces the support structure until it disappears entirely. These external scaffolds can be removed because the students have developed new cognitive processes that assist them in making connections between previously learned material and new knowledge. Students have discovered a "need" to know, a method to ensure they understand the information, and a "use" for the knowledge. The goal of scaffolding is to allow students to do as much as they can on their own and then to provide the necessary steps, tools, models, or practices for the students to become self-regulated independent learners.

In Chapter 7, a reference was made to the use of an outline to assist a person in writing a research paper. While a teacher may wish to see that an outline has been created and used, the outline itself is not the final product. It's a support structure that helps to organize ideas into an effective presentation. People who publish their reports, articles, and the like, do not publish the outline they used to assist them. The final product stands on its own legs.

Students should be aware that a support system is available when they need it. Learning has to be fun, challenging, relevant, and meaningful. There has to be an immediate use for the learning and a way to apply it in real-world situations. The learning must have a function; there must be a "need" to learn so that the mind can be engaged not only in ways to master the knowledge and skills but also in ways to use them. In that regard the teacher plays a pivotal role by encouraging, supporting, and modeling the learning through an active partnership with the student. The teacher must be willing to have a dialogue with students and must be sensitive about their needs, be able to show connections between the new and previous learning, be convinced that all students who are provided with enough time and support can learn, and be willing to accept initial errors as part of the growth process. The teacher must determine just how much support the student needs, as well as how and when to reduce that support as the student masters the learning. In addition, the teacher should know when to reintroduce the scaffold to sustain the learning.

Scaffolds help to do the following:

- Provide a motivation for a student to learn by tying in the new knowledge to present-day applications.

- Break down the task or assignment into workable, understandable parts.

- Provide a goal, an end point, so the students have a direction to follow.

- Provide assessment tools so the students can see where they are in relationship to the standard(s) being addressed.

- Reduce fear and frustration, and encourage risk taking.

- Provide models that demonstrate the expectations of the activity the students will undertake.

An honors science class was having difficulty solving a series of problems. When the teacher did the problems on the board, the students had no difficulty with the math. Puzzled, the teacher went to the English Department chairperson and asked for help. The solution was that the students were looking at the problems as a whole rather than as a series of parts. The English teacher created a graphic organizer that helped the students to split each of the problems into several key questions. By following the chain of specific questions that were being asked in the problem and answering each part separately, the students could put the pieces together into the correct answer for the whole problem. Some students continued to use the graphic organizer for longer than did others. Eventually, all of the students understood the structure of the problems sufficiently and were weaned off the support tools.

WHAT EVERYONE NEEDS TO KNOW

One of the key factors in using scaffolding is assessing the students so that the teacher knows who needs support and how much support a student needs at a given time. Similarly, knowing when to remove the support so that the student tries to apply the new knowledge and skills is equally important.

- Learning always begins from what is known to what is new, what is simple to what is complex.
- Teachers must identify student strengths so they can build upon them.
- The scaffold that the teacher provides may be different for each student; one size doesn't necessarily fit all.
- Scaffolding techniques are often not included in teacher guides or curriculum manuals; they require teacher analysis of individual student needs.
- Scaffolding is temporary and must be carefully removed as the student progresses to stages of understanding and application.
- Students must be encouraged and motivated to do as much as they can on their own before scaffolds are introduced.
- Teachers must manage time efficiently and effectively.
  - ○ More time is needed if the material is complex or completely unknown by the students.
  - ○ More time is needed if the students lack the basic ability to grasp or to apply the knowledge.
- Students should be matched to appropriate activities.
- The importance of learning the knowledge or skills must be demonstrated to students.
- Teachers must expect more errors at the beginning of the learning and provide redirection and feedback as needed.
- Time and opportunity for reflection allows students can privately internalize what is being taught.
- Instruction should move from teacher-directed to student-directed activities.
- The teacher must introduce steps that build upon the student's previous knowledge.
- The material to be presented should be broken up into manageable pieces.

- The teacher must continually check for individual understanding and make adjustments accordingly.
- Providing sufficient models and exemplars allows students to assess and adjust their progress toward the final goal.
- The teacher must make sure that the requirements of the lesson parallel requirements in real-world applications.
- Scaffolding tools must be appropriate to the task.

The process of scaffolding can be summed up in the following way: the teacher performs the activity and the student watches; next, the teacher performs the activity and the student assists; then the student performs the activity as the teacher assists; finally, the student performs the activity and the teacher watches. In this way, students get the support they need through the critical application phase and can correct and adjust their performance as necessary without the fear of failure.

TOOLS TO DEVELOP UNDERSTANDING

There are many tools that teachers and students can use to develop understanding. Some of these are more structured and require a precision that may appeal more to a scientific or mathematical mind that wants every detail included. Others are less formal and create an overall picture of relationships, which may be what the student needs to see the whole as the sum of its parts. Traditional outline formats are well known and widely used organizers that can be quite formal, depending on the degree of specificity required. For most people, anything beyond a two-level outline gets too complex for efficient use. Similarly, remembering all of the rules associated with the use of traditional outlines sometimes bogs down the focus of the lesson: providing support to the learner.

THE THREE P'S OF SCAFFOLDING PIECES: PROBLEMS, PROJECTS, AND PRESENTATIONS

The following graphic organizers (Figure 10.1) are a few of the more popular and easy to use scaffolding pieces, though they are not the only ones available. They range from the simple to the more complex and can be modified to fit the needs of the students. Likewise, they can be used in combinations to create simplicity in complex problems. The ultimate purpose is for these supports to be used by the students when and if they need to concentrate on the specific skills required in a lesson. The organizers allow students to use new sets of lenses in looking at the three P's: problems, projects, and presentations.

MODEL BEHAVIOR

Another scaffolding tool is a model, which can be used in two different ways. First, students may be given a model so they can see the connection between

Figure 10.1 Graphic Organizers

Venn Diagram

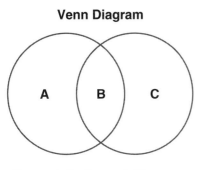

Shows similarities and differences.

Cycle

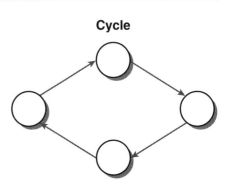

Shows how activities interact.

Step Chart

Steps	Details
1.	
2.	
3.	
4.	
5.	
6.	

Lists activities and the order in
which they should happen.

Series of Events

Starting Action
Event 1
Event 2
Final Result

Identifies a timeline

Continuum

Lists timelines, ratings, degrees of
accomplishment.

Compare/Contrast

	NAME 1	NAME 2
Feature 1		
Feature 2		
Feature 3		
Feature 4		

Shows areas of similarity and/or differences

Problem/Solution

Who What Why
Solutions
Results
End Result

Identifying problems, posing
solutions, analyzing results.

Spider Map

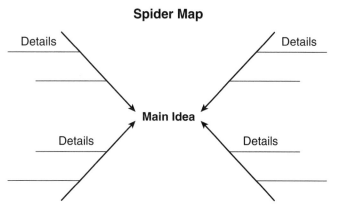

Describes a main idea through the use of details.

Knowledge Chart

What we know.	What we want to find out.	What we have learned.	How we'll use what we have learned.

Ties in previous information to present use.

Double Cell

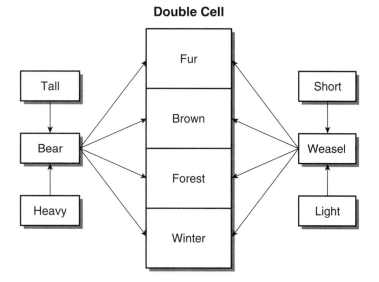

Shows individual as well as shared characteristics.

(Continued)

Figure 10.1 (Continued)

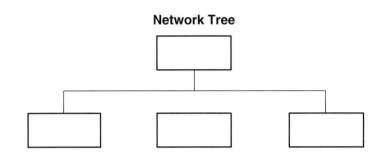

Network Tree

Shows an order in how things are related to each other.

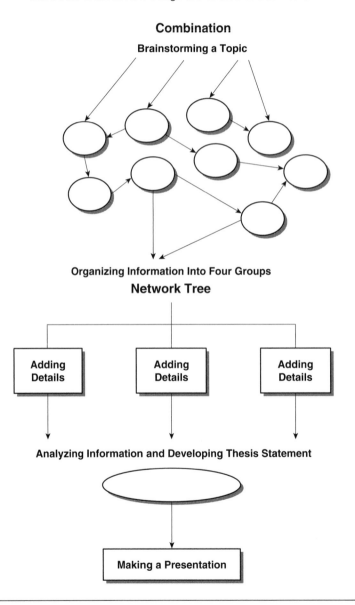

Combination

Brainstorming a Topic

Organizing Information Into Four Groups

Network Tree

| Adding Details | Adding Details | Adding Details |

Analyzing Information and Developing Thesis Statement

Making a Presentation

and among parts. Recently, a student from Iran moved to California. He listened to news broadcasts referring to Washington, the nation's capital, and the cherry blossoms. Months later, he heard people in supermarkets talking about the quality of cherries from Washington. To him, Washington, DC, was in the state of Washington, which was just north of California. When one of his teachers talked about scheduling an extended field trip to see the White House and Congress, he assumed that the class would be taking a bus. Only when the teacher brought out a map and a globe did he become aware of the difference between the two places geographically. The models showed him the locations and the relative distances.

Second, students may create a model from component parts to see what something would look like in its entirety before going ahead with the project. Many decorating consultants have computer software that allows them to create virtual reality models; they can see how changing walls, doors, or windows impacts space. They create the model to assess the project before actually ripping out existing structures. In both cases, models act as scaffolds or support tools to enhance understanding.

- A model is a representation depicting a simplified way in which the material world may be viewed.

- A model may be an exact copy or a representation of reality.
  o Physical model (model that can be manipulated)
  o Visual model (3-D image, pattern)

- A model may be a representation of an idea.
  o Mathematical model (charts)

- A model may be used to describe, explain, predict, develop, or test ideas.
  o Statistical model (graphs)

The grid in Figure 10.2 points out different types of models, as well as the ways students might use them as support pieces.

The rubric in Figure 10.3 can be used for self-assessment.

Figure 10.2 Scaffolding Tool for Model Use

TYPE OF MODEL	PURPOSE OF MODEL	STUDENT USE
Exact Copy	Useful for seeing parts.	Student is unable to manipulate the model to see why certain parts are more important than others.
Representation, Illustration of Reality	Useful for illustrating a process.	Student uses the model only as a reference and can't critique the model.
Abstraction	Useful for thinking about a structure, idea, theory, or process.	Student uses the model to adapt and evaluate ideas that the model represents.

Figure 10.3 Scaffolding Rubric for the Teacher

Level of Performance: 4 = Advanced, 3 = Proficient, 2 = Average, 1 = Needs Improvement

SCAFFOLDING RUBRIC	4	3	2	1
Students are assessed for prior knowledge.				
Teacher has identified the modifications necessary to involve all of the learners.				
Sequence of lesson moves from teacher-directed to student-directed.				
Sequence of lessons moves from simple tasks to more difficult ones.				
Activity utilizes scaffolding strategies.				
Activity utilizes modeling strategies.				
Activity utilizes guided examples prior to students undertaking independent work.				
Requirements in the directed activity parallel requirements in the independent practice.				

SAMPLE LESSON WITH SCAFFOLDING

Consider the following assignment:

> After reading *Lord of the Flies* by William Golding and seeing how the dark side of humanity emerged on the island, write an essay dealing with four major needs that the boys lacked that caused them to descend into the depths of depravity. Show how these four needs had a direct bearing on the boys' inability to maintain basic laws of civilization. Provide details from the novel to support your choices.

For some students, this topic may be overwhelming. Consider what is required:

1. What are some basic laws of civilization that the boys broke?

2. What are examples of the "dark side of humanity" that the boys exhibited?

3. What are four major needs for the boys and are these needs the same for the different age ranges of the boys?
   a. Are these material needs, such as clothing or supplies?
   b. Are these companionship needs, such as having girls or adults on the island to act as stabilizing forces?
   c. Are these spiritual or psychological needs?

4. How does the lack of these areas directly impact the boys?
    a. What incidents or interactions show this the best?
    b. What are the best examples from the novel to support each choice?
    c. How many examples should be used to support each choice?

5. How will the thesis statement reflect what is required in this essay?

Include questions that involve the structure of the completed essay as well as the mechanics that go into writing it, and one can see that this task could prove difficult to some students at first glance. Now, scaffolding strategies enter.

(1.) Acting as a facilitator and a transcriber on the board, the teacher brainstorms, with the entire class, the basic laws of a civilized society, making sure to distinguish between a written law and an unwritten law.

(2.) Looking at the list, the teacher and students try to arrive at categories under which some of the items on the list may fit (e.g., laws involving physical safety, social comfort, educational progress, spiritual growth). These may be listed under a network tree graphic organizer to give students a sensory image.

(3.) Students then have to create criteria to judge which four of these categories are the most important and which entries within each category are most compelling. Students edit out the weaker details.

(4.) Students can then be broken up into smaller groups in which each group brainstorms occasions when the boys descend into the "dark side of humanity." Again, students create categories, sort, and edit. All the time, the teacher goes from group to group motivating and providing feedback.

(5.) Some students might then be able to use a spider map, a problem/solution graphic, or a double cell to create a visual picture of how these two areas of civilization and the lack of civilization coincide and conflict. Those students who are still having difficulty can continue working with the teacher with additional steps or organizers. As the students reach a comfort range, the "I got it" stage, they drop from the group and continue on individually addressing the topic.

In short, the organizers help the students to divide the topic into manageable questions that they can investigate. Once they have all of the pieces, they can put them together into a thesis statement and an outline and then can proceed to tackle the entire problem posed by the question.

The checklist in Figure 10.4 is provided for parents to use to determine ways that they can become active partners with the students.

Learning does not begin or end at the schoolhouse door. Parents have to be vital partners in the community of learning and should practice with the students the strategies that the schools teach. Scaffolding is an important strategy because it is easily applied to countless real-world problem-solving situations. Parents can motivate their children by showing them the immediate value of what they are learning and instances where they can apply the learning meaningfully. Have students schedule places to visit on the next family vacation; list the

ideas to give students to aid in development

steps necessary to teach a younger sibling a basic skill; show someone how to follow a recipe; chart ways to grocery shop more efficiently; list and prioritize escape routes from the home in case of emergency; create a nutrition chart for someone in the family to lose weight safely; chart a family exercise program based on the time availability of each family member; chart spending habits and problem solve ways for the family to save money for the next vacation.

WHAT MOST PEOPLE NEED TO KNOW

To assess the students and provide the appropriate scaffolding strategies that are necessary, the teacher first has to be a content expert in the grade-level subject matter. Reading a chapter ahead of the students or relying on teachers' textbook answer sheets in order to address problem-solving situations in the classroom creates an environment of uncertainty for both the teacher and the students. Overcoming poor content knowledge is the responsibility of the teacher, but detecting areas of deficiency falls upon the middle manager, whose role is to provide the teacher with support and direct the educator to immediate assistance through professional development. A person who is trying to survive intellectually can't be expected to have the time or the skill to provide support for students. Scaffolding is an important tool that not only increases student understanding but also motivates the students to learn. Used by a content expert, scaffolding can greatly increase the ability of students to understand and to solve complex issues by allowing them to concentrate on what is actually required to succeed.

- Teachers need to be held accountable as content experts so they can provide the scaffolding tools necessary for individual students to use in specific situations.

- Professional development must include not only methodology but also content reinforcement, class management, and organization skill development.

- Middle managers need to schedule faculty, department, or grade-level meetings to discuss and share problem-solving techniques, time management strategies, and lesson design that includes scaffolding.

- Teachers need access to graphic organizer templates and models (e.g., globes, charts, graphs, pictures, tapes) as well as to the equipment necessary to show these models in the most effective light.

- Teachers need a flexible use of space to accommodate peer and group learning situations. Proper scheduling makes this happen.

- Teachers need to be trained to use effective brainstorming techniques to encourage students to have the idea base to use organizational tools.

- Teacher plan books need to be checked frequently to determine not only lesson design but also scaffolding strategies.

- Teachers should be encouraged to post lessons on the Web and show scaffolding tools associated with the lessons.

Figure 10.4   Scaffolding Checklist for Parents

PARENT CHECKLIST	YES	NO
I understand the importance of using scaffolding strategies in the classroom and at home.		
I understand how and when to use graphic organizers.		
I add more examples or model the skill/learning my child needs to progress.		
I encourage my child to apply schoolhouse learning/problem-solving strategies to real-life situations occurring in and around my household.		
I act as a learner and have my child explain the use of organizers to me.		
I encourage my child to help in family brainstorming sessions by acting as a facilitator, a contributor, or a transcriber.		
I try to sequence learning tasks from being directed solely by me to being student driven.		
I try to use a nonlecture approach with much hands-on application.		
I encourage my child to use a variety of organizational strategies in problem-solving situations.		
I provide support for my child to receive feedback on errors and make corrections and adjustments.		
I communicate to the teacher any difficulties my child has in interpreting, understanding, and completing assignments or in using scaffolding.		
I help my child to use the rubrics and assessment tools associated with the lesson.		
I show my child the relationship of the learning to the standard being covered and reinforce the importance of the learning.		
I try to show my child that learning, although work, can be fun.		
I try to have my child use previous learning to make connections to new knowledge and skills.		
I try to work with my child's strengths to ensure success.		

- Committees of grade-level teachers and managers should be organized and should meet regularly to create scaffolding tools to complement textbook and Web lessons.

WHAT SOME PEOPLE NEED TO KNOW

- Administrators should be aware of the value of these organizational pieces throughout the education process. They should provide the means for teachers, students, and parents to have greater accessibility to them.

- Parents must be provided with a list of scaffolding strategies, complete with instructions for their use, so they can use them at home with their students. These may be included in such things as newsletters and brochures that are provided by the school district.

- Student handbooks should contain organizational tools for use by students in various problem-solving situations.

- All teachers need to be provided with a districtwide list of professionally made teaching models designated by grade level.

- Districts should coordinate the purchase of professionally made visual, physical, or statistical models to ensure that needless duplication doesn't occur. Sufficient numbers of models should be available to meet the needs of multiple classrooms; all subject areas benefit.

SUMMARY

Scaffolding is an important tool that can both support and motivate students to succeed. Teachers must know when to use it and also when to withdraw it. They must be selective in knowing what scaffolding students need at the appropriate time.

- The best learning is fun if it is challenging, relevant, useful, and supported to make it successful.

- All students can learn given enough time, motivation, a supportive environment, and the necessary supplemental tools.

- Scaffolding should proceed from teacher-directed as student watches, to teacher-directed and student assists, to student-directed and teacher assists, and finally to student-directed and teacher watches activities. Substitute parent for teacher in the home educational environment.

- Scaffolding reduces frustration, provides organized direction for the student to achieve the goal, and sets a tone for success.

- Scaffolding builds upon a student's prior knowledge, the ability to make connections with new learning, and focuses on the student's strengths.

- Scaffolding is temporary and leaves when the "I got it" phase enters.

Instructional Grouping 11

In the traditional school, grouping often meant students were alphabetically arranged, sitting in uniform rows, all facing forward toward the teacher and the board. For a straight lecture format, this pattern probably fits the bill as well as anything else. But, since every class wasn't a lecture, this format worked only part of the time. Occasionally, a teacher recognized this fact and tried to do something about it by grouping students in other ways. Unfortunately, as long as the class was easily divisible by two, these new groupings generally consisted of pairings; if there were an odd number of students, trios usually fit the bill. However, even though the grouping was different, it failed because students went into groups to do "something," and then came out of the group to hand in an individual or group product. The result was that individual accountability within the group wasn't considered a high priority as long as "work" was done.

So, despite the fact that the teacher was able to break away from the original "row mentality," this technique proved just as bad because, instead of monitoring the progress of students, the major concern was now focused on not disturbing the row structure. Thus, students were monitored as they put back desks and chairs on precise dots or lines on the floor almost in fear that the janitor was going to rush in and reprimand them if everything wasn't exactly as it had been. The consequence was that, almost to a person, as each student entered the new pairing or trio, the first thing they'd ask one another would be, "Do you know what we're supposed to do?" When nobody knew, the follow-up question, "What do you want me to do," was directed at the teacher. In the midst of this confusion, the teacher was usually wandering around the room trying to assess the situation. Eventually, frustrated by the lack of progress and the continual barrage of questions, the teacher would stop the action, go to the chalkboard and, in a loud voice, announce, "Okay, I want you to stop what you're doing and pay attention to me. Most of you. . . ." The remainder of the sentence usually pointed out what the students weren't doing and tried to explain what they should be doing. Yet it still gave little or no guidance as to how the students could assess their own performance, nor did it establish roles in the group. In short, if the students didn't know where they were going, any road would do.

If there was no need for specific grouping, why do it? The work product was no better, student behavior worsened, and it required an effort that the traditional row grouping did not. In other words, the problems (students, receiving imprecise directions and goals, usually lapsed into boredom or "acting up" patterns) often outweighed the advantages. This is only because the entire process was done incorrectly. Recent studies have shown that instructional grouping, if used constructively, does have advantages, especially in preparing students to understand the dynamics of problem solving in real-world situations. Students build the social skills necessary to assist them in utilizing the intellectual skills they must use in the present and the future.

Keeping in mind that instructional grouping really can work, the first order of business is to figure out the best way to use groupings. In this regard, it's important to recognize that all classrooms are generally designed around three types of thinking: competition, individuality, and cooperation. Before deciding on a particular type of grouping, the teacher must examine the three types of classroom configurations.

Since most of the outside world stresses competition, this characteristic is easy to carry over into the school. Most students automatically feel they have to compete against their classmates, and often take great care not to share anything that might give another student any advantage. Often parents and schools encourage this notion by constantly comparing student achievement to other students in the class; schools do it with valedictorian status awarded to the top student. The only problem with this scenario is that one person wins and all of the other people lose. Thus, the flaw in this system appears in the lesser-gifted students, those who never have the chance of being the best, as they often lose focus when they cannot remain competitive. Still, competition can't be dismissed altogether because it does possess the virtue of motivating students to rise above the average.

The second category, individuality, is one in which the students perform work for self-satisfaction; consequently, they're not as concerned with how it fits into the entire spectrum. These are generally grade-oriented individuals who really don't pay much attention to the others in the class and who work toward an established set of criteria. As a result, the success or failure of other students in the classroom doesn't affect their scores or standings. Unfortunately, the problem with this system is that, again, some students progress while others don't. In addition, the social skills that are necessary in the real world aren't adequately developed.

The third category, cooperation, represents the ideal grouping wherein students are working together in a positive goal-interdependence, but they have individual accountability added. In other words, each individual in the group is accountable to the success of the group as a whole. The whole group can achieve more than can the singularly competitive or the individual student because it brings more resources together. Likewise, students have more opportunities to assess their contributions in light of their peers so they are constantly correcting and adjusting.

GROUPING DEFINED

What! In an educational setting, grouping occurs when a large body of students is broken down into smaller groups for some or all of the time that the students are in the classroom. For as long as they last, each smaller group is treated as a separate, but equal, social and educational unit. The groups, either as a whole or as individual entities, are provided with a clear objective. They are also supplied with assessments, which allow them to gauge when, and to what degree, they have achieved the objective. The result is that although the students have roles and accountability as individuals within the group, the final product is a group "sink or swim" effort.

Why: One of the key ways that students reinforce their learning and skills and succeed is because they have to teach others in their group. Statistics show that the highest retention comes from having to teach something to someone else (see Figure 8.1). The group dynamic offers these opportunities multiple times within a single project. In addition, grouping helps to develop interpersonal skills that are necessary to share information in real-world settings. Likewise, the group gives individuals the opportunity to exercise the higher order thinking skills of synthesis and evaluation.

When: Students may be brought together to provide support for each other involving a project. They may be given opportunities to engage in enrichment activities, allocated time to practice content and skills covered in the lesson, engaged in problem-solving exercises, or even provided opportunities for brainstorming sessions.

WHAT EVERYONE NEEDS TO KNOW

While grouping can be a highly effective method of increasing educational opportunities for students, teachers must be careful not to use it indiscriminately. Grouping should not be automatic for each lesson, but used when active learning can proceed more effectively. Likewise, it's not a substitute for teaching nor is it to be used for "downtime" purposes.

Grouping is not meant to accomplish the following:

- Asking the students who have mastered the standards to spend all of their time in assisting students who are having difficulty

- Grouping students in such a way that one person does the work and everyone else copies the results

- Having students doing relative but not relevant work

- Rewarding a group when not all students contributed

- Allowing random selection in the grouping process

- Assuming that social skills have been learned and are being utilized

- Using unstructured group processing roles and strategies

- Using fixed, long-term groups only

- Using typically large groups (more than five members)

- Releasing the teacher from active involvement

- Focusing only on the end product and not on the process

Grouping, as a tool, can be a highly effective teaching strategy, as it promotes not only educational but also social relationship rewards. Students learn and apply those skills necessary to provide positive interaction with each other. Students are placed into situations that more closely represent real-world application scenarios; they develop an understanding of both individual accountability as well as the team concept. They are placed in situations in which not only the teacher but also their peers can help them correct and adjust in a less stressful atmosphere.

Grouping is meant to accomplish the following:

- Assuring that all students are involved in the learning
- Increasing student involvement in the process of learning, as well as in the learning product itself
- Teaching students how to interact with other people
- Teaching students how to learn by adopting and formulating various strategies
- Teaching students to act interdependently but with individual accountability
- Teaching students leadership, trust building, communication, and conflict management skills

GROUPING SIZE

The size of a group matters significantly, as does its composition. Teachers must take these factors into account and not just create groups that are easily divided by a set core number.

In a large group, the slower-processing students may need more time to attain a specific objective since their interaction within the group may be limited by their need to deal with the material or assignment at a slower pace. They could get overlooked by more rapid-processing students and their contributions or learning could be diminished.

In a small group, the slower-processing students have more time to receive instruction and immediate support. Short-term, small instructional groups generally provide the students with more opportunity for review, practice, and enrichment. There is additional opportunity for more students to provide explanations, demonstrations, and strategies for new learning. Slower-achieving students usually spend more time on task in small groups since they wait less time for instructions and feedback from their peers and the teacher.

Cooperative group experiences generally increase the achievements of female students more than male students. See Chapter 12, "Brain-Based Learning," in which studies show that female students process information faster and communicate more openly than do male students.

Using small groups may help to eliminate student cliques since all students rotate within groups and are interacting with each other and not just within select groups. Long-term grouping tends to have adverse effects on slower-achieving students since they have a tendency to get locked in to specific roles within the group. The chart in Figure 11.1 demonstrates the criteria associated with peer pairs, grouping investigations, and open-ended groupings.

The chart in Figure 11.2 represents the group type, the reason for using this particular grouping, the advantages associated with this type of grouping, and the disadvantages that might impede its use. For example, the use of two students requires more materials (such as handouts, computers, printers, scissors, and paper) than would a larger group. Where school supplies are in great demand, the two-student grouping might quickly deplete resources. Twenty-four students in 12 two-student combinations sharing a handout sheet and a computer require 12 handout sheets and 12 computers; 24 students in six larger groups sharing resources would require six handouts and six computers. Since many classrooms across the country are limited in the number of computer terminals available, the larger grouping scenario might be a better alternative in some learning situations.

For purposes of clarification, a *two-student group* is composed of two students who work together to assist each other in finding an agreed upon solution or in practicing a skill. Their results are given to the teacher. A *two-student share team* is composed of two students who are asked to think about a topic, work with their partner to discuss their thinking or ideas, and present their findings to the class. A *student teaching pair* involves each of the duo instructing the other member in applying the skill that the lesson objective identifies. Students assess each other as they practice the skill. *Jigsaw* is a grouping strategy in which students work in six-member teams on an academic project, which has been broken down into sections for each member. The remaining configurations generally have established roles within the grouping structure.

Certain room space doesn't easily accommodate some of the larger groupings, as desks and work space intrude on other groups. Likewise, small groups may take up such space as to prevent the teacher from going around and interacting. Having to move desks and chairs around and back may take up valuable

Figure 11.1 Group Composition and Time

TWO STUDENTS	THREE TO FOUR STUDENTS	FIVE OR MORE STUDENTS
The group work is short, lasting part of a period to two days.	The group work can cover a few days to a few weeks.	The group work can cover days or weeks.
The task is limited (usually practice or review).	Each student has a clearly defined role in reaching a performance objective that has been defined by the teacher.	The objective is open-ended, may involve multiple standards, and may be generated within the group.
Students assess themselves and each other.	All team members must contribute.	Student roles are flexible and are dictated by the process of reaching the objective.
Each student can offer a strategy to explain the results.	The end product represents the work of the entire group.	The end product represents the work of the entire group.
The students share their results with the class.	Cooperation in the group is part of the learning process.	The students share their product with the other groups.

Figure 11.2 Teacher Reference List for Grouping

GROUP TYPE	NUMBER	TIME	REASON	ADVANTAGES	DISADVANTAGES
Two Students	2 people	1–2 days	Review, practice, drill	Flexible, easily set up	Need materials for each pair, difficult to monitor
Two-Student Share	2 people	1 day	Brainstorming, organizing, presenting	Flexible, easily set up	Need materials for each pair, difficult to monitor
Student Teaching Pair	2 people	1–2 days	Practice, reinforcement, review	Flexible, easily set up	Need materials for each pair, difficult to monitor
Jigsaw	4–5 people	1 day–2 weeks	Individual research but group product	Teaches social skills, total student involvement	Space, supplementary resources
Group Investigation	4–5 people	1 day–2 weeks	Group research and group product	Teaches social skills, total student involvement	Space, supplementary resources
Open-Ended Group	4–5 people	3 days–2 weeks	Open-ended research with individual and collaborative products	Flexible roles, teaches social skills, total student involvement	Space, supplementary resources, conflict management, difficult to monitor
Long-Term Group	4–5 people	2+ weeks	Introduce, practice, review, reinforce	Deals with specific needs	Students become locked into roles
Total Class Group	All students	1–2 days	Introduce, review, test	Works best with lecture and formal testing; most effective use of space	Difficult to monitor, need multiple materials, difficult to assess

class time; therefore, the teacher has to plan out in advance the benefits that each grouping design brings and the disadvantages it outweighs.

There are additional information pieces about grouping strategies that are important and that everyone needs to know. Some of them address the space considerations necessary for groups to function, while other pieces deal with times that the teacher must intervene to keep students moving on relevant rather than relative tracks.

- Small group members have to be close together and facing each other in order to promote communication.

- The groups must be arranged so that the teacher and other groups have easy physical access to each other.

- Relevant materials have to be easily accessible for each group to use.

- Each group must be provided with a group objective as well as a specific description of the necessary task to complete that goal.

- Assessment pieces should be available to each group so that members can adjust their own performance as well as that of the group.

- The teacher, in conjunction with the students, must establish the criteria necessary to ensure that everyone understands the basic behaviors that define cooperation in and between groups.

- The teacher must monitor the groups.
  - Introduce new material as needed.
  - Determine what skills are lacking and need to be introduced.
  - Determine what skills are necessary and need to be reinforced or reviewed.
  - Intervene when major problems arise.
  - Rearrange the composition of groups as needed.
  - Regulate the time on task.
  - Define group roles and responsibilities.

Grouping allows the teacher to monitor and check to see that the work of the group, as well as the individual members of the group, is proceeding efficiently and effectively (see Figure 11.3).

The template in Figure 11.4 has been designed to address a teacher's need to organize information about grouping. It provides a lens for the teacher to use to see whether the objective of the class would best be served by grouping the students into a cooperative configuration. Likewise, the teacher can anticipate possible problems and brainstorm potential solutions.

SO, WHAT IF GROUPING STRATEGIES ARE NOT WORKING? JUMP SHIP OR ROW TO SHORE?

"The best laid schemes o' mice an' men gang aft agley [often go awry]" is not only a key line from Robert Burns's work, but it also serves as the partial title of a John Steinbeck novel. The lesson to be learned is that not everything runs as smoothly as it was designed or planned. While some teachers may have tremendous success in trying all of these strategies, other instructors may have comfort with using only two or three. The solution lies in not forcing grouping strategies on situations that don't call for them, and in recognizing potential problems *before* they occur. In this way the teacher can brainstorm possible solutions, employ differentiation or scaffolding strategies to overcome the obstacles, or modify and clarify assessment resources. The template in Figure 11.5 lists some of the possible problems that might occur in implementing grouping situations and offers some possible solutions. Correcting a problem in a two-student group or a two-student share is often easier to do than having to engage larger grouping formation difficulties; however, this isn't meant to discourage their use among teachers.

Planning grouping strategies in advance, thinking out advantages and disadvantages, and not just deciding at the spur of the moment to group is probably the best way to ensure success. "Hey, I just got an idea. Let's break up into groups," is

Figure 11.3   Teacher Checklist for Grouping

PREPARATION	YES	NO
Have I determined that the objective could best be attained through the use of grouping?		
Have I determined the type of grouping that will be necessary for the students to achieve the objective?		
Have I used the necessary strategies to determine which students will be in each group?		
Have I provided a clear explanation of the tasks and expectations to be completed by each group and by each member of the group?		
Have I provided for the physical layout of the room to promote cooperation, access, and communication?		
Have I provided sufficient materials and resources for each group?		
Have I clearly defined student roles within each group?		
Have I instructed students on the social skills necessary to operate within a group structure?		
Have I provided assessment pieces so members may monitor both individual and group performance?		
Have I provided the scaffolding for each group and each member of the group to reach the objective?		
Have I provided differentiation methods to engage all of the students all of the time?		
Have I provided sufficient time for students and groups to meet the objective?		
Have I provided ongoing feedback so that groups can correct and adjust?		
Have I used the method of presentation of the group product as a learning tool for the class?		
Have I addressed student learning and presentation styles in the performance objective and in the presentation of the product?		

probably a strong signal that the grouping activity may achieve less than satisfactory results. "Form your own groups" probably is not going to accomplish either the educational nor social expectations that could be achieved from preplanning.

WHAT MOST PEOPLE NEED TO KNOW

For teachers to learn the ins and outs of new ideas on grouping and become comfortable enough with the concepts to use them in everyday classroom situations, middle managers must take a proactive approach toward getting across the fundamentals of these techniques. This can occur in a number of ways. For

Figure 11.4   Group Design Template

Class:	
Beginning Date:	
Standards:	
Performance Objectives:	

Group Type/Size: **Differentiation:**	**Required Roles:**
Potential Problems:	**Scaffolding:**
Possible Solutions:	

instance, several department heads can cooperate to train their combined departments by scheduling a joint workshop. They can then divide the teachers into small groups made up of individuals from different departments and give them a preset objective and preset assessments. The result is that the workshop produces a twofold benefit. First, training goals are met and teachers learn valuable skills that they can take into the classroom. Second, by participating in the training rather than merely observing, teachers gain firsthand knowledge of the usefulness of grouping. However, for middle managers to introduce grouping ideas properly, they must be familiar with the following and must provide solutions to address these potential problems.

- Because most teachers have been taught using traditional learning groups (full class or long-term groups), they need specific training in the management, organization, monitoring, and implementation of grouping as an educational tool.

- Collegial time is necessary for teachers to share experiences, discuss results, and compare strategies with peers and mentors.

Figure 11.5   Troubleshooting Grouping Problems

PROBLEM	POSSIBLE SOLUTION
All students are not actively engaged or work is proceeding slowly.	Assign specific tasks to the students: • accuracy checker • materials supplier • record keeper • time-keeper • liaison to other groups
Students are acting up.	• Provide differentiation. • Provide scaffolding steps. • Recheck the composition of the group. • Use accountability motivation. • Check the physical spacing between groups. • Reinforce social skills involving cooperation and communication. • Provide more immediate feedback. • Adjust the time for completion of the objective. • Adjust the presentation of the product.
Groups are too noisy.	• Adjust the spacing between groups. • Adjust the spacing within the groups. • Reinforce social skills involving communication and cooperation.
Students are working against each other within the group.	• Reinforce/review methods of conflict management. • Adjust the composition of the group.
The quality of work is deteriorating.	• Reinforce/review use of assessment tools. • Provide reflection time so students/groups can make connection with the learning. • Monitor the group more closely with frequent checks for understanding. • Have groups check in with each other more often. • Provide additional resources.

- Teachers need to create and share common assessment tools.

- Teachers need training in classroom management and conflict resolution as they apply to grouping.

- A list of supplementary resource materials and equipment in the school or district will help teachers facilitate research within the groups.

- Teachers need training in providing differentiation strategies between groups.

- Training teachers in designing scaffolding steps to be used within and between groups is also necessary.

- Teachers must have the opportunity to apply their learning by interacting in grouping environments during grade-level, department, or faculty meetings, as well as during training sessions.

WHAT SOME PEOPLE NEED TO KNOW

Most principals and superintendents are not involved in the day-to-day decision making that occurs in the classroom, so their role is to provide those resources (such as budget, professional development, and access to time) that are necessary to ensure the success of grouping strategies. Professional development, using grouping as an educational tool, needs to be built in to budgetary and time considerations for school or district professional development days. Mentoring teachers in the use of grouping should be explored as a district goal.

SUMMARY

Grouping is a strategy that, when used properly, can enhance a learner's sense of accomplishment and self-esteem. It can also immerse the learner in those types of real-world problem-solving situations that occur constantly inside and outside of the classroom.

- Short-term grouping provides more opportunity to emphasize the student as learner rather than the teacher as teacher.

- Grouping encourages students to teach each other.

- Small groups allow slower-achieving students more opportunity for immediate feedback.

12 Brain-Based Learning

Brain-based learning is an understanding of learning based on the structure and function of the brain. Learning occurs if the brain is not inhibited by factors such as fear and stress. In recent years, many educators have been fascinated by the new brain research in the hopes that it will lead to significant discoveries about the way people learn. Some neuroscientists are ready to claim that the brain works like a computer that collects, processes, creates, stores, and manipulates the information it receives; but other scientists feel the brain is more like a jungle with a tangled maze of interdependent connections that function on an incalculable number of variations (Jensen, 1998). Debate persists about when neuron connections are made and when to introduce certain aspects of learning in children to achieve optimum success.

While brain-based learning may seem to be an unusual topic in a book devoted to standards-based teaching, in actuality, this chapter's purpose is to reinforce strategies the teacher can employ to ensure the success of the standards-based model. Many people advocate a total adoption of the brain-based system, but this chapter addresses only those elements of brain research that have been proven in testing or in practical application.

Teachers need to understand that students work more efficiently and effectively when the brain can make connections between previously learned and new material, when the pupils can see patterns develop in order to establish meaning. Likewise, instructors must be aware of the differences between how females and males process and communicate information, how the brain perceives threat versus challenge, and how punishment and reward systems really work. In addition, teachers should understand the need for providing organizational structures inherent for students to understand specific subject areas. Teachers who have been schooled using traditional rote memorization techniques need to understand the limitations of this method. Also, they must be cognizant of the basics involving body movement and learning, proper brain hydration, and the effects of sleep deprivation or lack of rest on a student's performance. Simple matters such as wait time or reflection must be factored in to give students opportunities to integrate their learning, to make it meaningful, and to provide opportunities for successful application in multiple settings. All of these factors work together to prepare the teacher to employ multiple strategies to promote student learning. All of the researchers agree that the brain is a highly complex organism that requires much more research before definitive findings can be used to pinpoint specific methods to increase learning.

How then can education profit from the research that has already been done? One of the recommendations is in creating the proper atmosphere in the classroom so the brain can be at its optimum for learning. A relaxed but focused setting, devoid of fear and stress, offers students options for learning in individually satisfying ways and increases their ability to build new understandings based on their prior experiences. Learning is enhanced by challenge and risk taking, but is inhibited by threat. Fear puts the brain into a survival mode, where it functions to forget more than to learn. In this state the brain struggles to operate in a basic mode to ensure its survival. It actually ceases risk taking and challenge, fearing those conditions will expose the person to increased threat. Instinct can overwhelm reason. In a secure setting where stress and threat are lowered but where positive interaction is encouraged and modeled, the brain accepts the challenge and begins the process of transferring new information into the application phase. In a standards-based classroom, the learner needs this positive stimulation minus the threat of failure associated with the traditional approach.

WHAT EVERYONE NEEDS TO KNOW

Many jokes conclude with the line that "you don't have to be a brain surgeon to. . . ." The reason this profession is chosen is that it typifies excellence and complexity of thought and skill, and deals with the core of the body's existence. The brain is an intricate organ that is undergoing constant exploration and analysis, not only for its cellular aspects but also for the way it functions in various circumstances and modes of operation.

- The two types of memory are *spatial,* which records daily experiences, and *rote,* which deals with facts and skills in isolation. Separating information and skills from previous experiences forces the learner to depend on rote memory, which ignores the learner's personality and probably interferes with the development of understanding. Rote memorization may be helpful sometimes (memorizing a multiplication table or a list of atomic weights), but it doesn't easily allow the transfer of learning or the application of new information. Likewise, it ignores the personal learning style of the student and actually may impede the effective functioning of the brain.

- The brain simultaneously sees and creates parts and wholes, and benefits more when information is presented in context rather than in isolation.

- The brain picks up signals about the value of information it receives from the enthusiasm, modeling, and coaching of the presenter. The teacher's style of presentation greatly affects the learning capacity of students.

- Punishment systems generally don't work on the brain.
  - They set up fear-induced situations that slow or stop learning from taking place. People become frozen into immobility by the perceived threat.

- They don't stop the offensive behavior but cause the learner to think of ways to avoid being caught the next time.

- Rules come with punishment, not rewards. In our society, the emphasis is not on reward for obeying the rules; it's on punishment if you violate them. The IRS, for example, has never rewarded anyone for years of paying taxes on time but is quick to prosecute people who fail to meet the obligation only once. Rules, then, are traditionally used to induce fear of punishment. The objective is not to get rid of rules; instead, it is to <u>change the mind-set to show that following rules contributes to success, which is rewarded.</u>

- Stress and threat affect the brain differently from challenge, happiness, and stability.

- Health management must be incorporated into the learning process: the body requires movement within 37-minute periods (Weiss, 2001); proper sleep and rest are essential; the brain must be hydrated during the day with water to increase or to maintain learning (Hannaford, 1995).

- The learning environment needs to provide stability and familiarity, but at the same time needs to create an atmosphere in which students can satisfy themselves with novelty, discovery, and challenge.

- The search for meaning occurs as the brain recognizes patterns (the meaningful organization and categorization of information). Meaningless patterns (isolated or unrelated bits of information) don't make sense to the brain and cause confusion. Patterning helps the brain to retain information based on a personal need.

- Emotions are critical to patterning. They help the mind to organize information based on relevancy and personal need. Often, when a teacher introduces the relative (nice but not important to know) information, the student becomes confused because the brain attempts to tie this information into the learning patterns it has already created. The learning goes off on a tangential plane, and the student has to struggle to make sense of where this piece fits into the whole.

- Many subject areas are best understood and mastered when they are involved in genuine experiences or in the context of application in real-world scenarios.

- Learning involves both conscious attention and subconscious perception. While the brain takes in information with which it is immediately involved, it also responds to information outside the direct involvement field (e.g., posters, art, musical pieces—which all serve to stimulate the brain).

- Processing time and reflection (thinking about what we know and what we don't know) are vital to creating a successful learning environment. Often, much teaching and studying time is used ineffectively since students don't adequately process their information and experiences, nor do they reflect back on the patterning they have created. This is why teachers have to provide time for students to process questions, as well as time to formulate answers. The first hand up in the room doesn't always indicate the smartest individual, as other students may be processing the information more thoroughly for a more complete response. Think back to most classroom situations. The teacher calls on the first person and is rarely satisfied that the answer of that individual is so complete that the lesson can move on. Instead, additional ideas are sought until the teacher and the class recognize that the subject has been resolved to everyone's satisfaction.

- The brain understands best when facts and skills require the use of multiple senses. Success in learning generally occurs when the students depend on using all of their senses while being immersed in a variety of complex, interactive experiences.

Multiple Senses

- A lecture can be used, but only as part of a more complete experience and not as the final entity in itself.

Think of experiences you had in school. If there was a threat of failure, of not passing, then you probably reacted in one of two ways: you gave up and accepted your fate, figuring you had no opportunity to pass so why continue to struggle; or you were so panicked that you rationalized ways to pass (e.g., copying someone else's homework, cramming for a test without really learning the material, or asking your parents to intercede with the teacher). In both cases, the threat produced a "no learning" situation as well as a lowering of self-esteem, and these results often carried themselves over into the future.

What was even worse was a teacher who punished or threatened a whole class for the failure or behavior of a few students. The thinking was that an overall threat would push certain students to perform and would keep those students who were performing in line. Although logical educators could quickly see this strategy's flaws, to this day these same threats of failure are used in classrooms around the country as intended motivating agents.

- The more the brain learns, the more experiences it has, the more individual it becomes. Since learners are all distinctive, they must be given choices that challenge them and cause them to use the information in their own personal and real-world settings.

- Students learn by doing. They require immediate feedback so they can correct errors and can build positive experiences to apply to new learning.

- The main principle of the brain is survival. The brain is constructed to forget or disregard those things that appear to have nothing to do with its survival or with the survival of the species. The teacher must create an environment that motivates the brain into getting past this bottom-line stage and into one that requires the brain to feel safe enough to take controlled risks. The teacher must maintain a level of interest rather than a level of stress.

- Science and math curricula have a different organizational scheme for understanding than do English and foreign language. Students must be given the organizing properties for each subject area so they can practice and apply the knowledge correctly. Any teacher can tell that science and math students are taught to be clear, specific, and succinct in their answers, whether written or oral. English and social studies students are taught to expand, amplify, and explain their answers using examples and figures of speech. Often, tests that are designed and corrected by a math teacher have different expectations than those created by an English instructor. Students can be easily confused when their answer is too brief in one class and too wordy in another. The role of the teacher is to make absolutely sure that students clearly understand and can apply the criteria, the organizing properties, of one discipline versus another.

THE MALE AND FEMALE BRAINS

Recent research has shown that the brains of men and women differ, so the teacher should be aware of this in order to address specific issues (James, 2007).

- Women are more in touch with their feelings and generally can express them better than do men.

- Women have an increased ability to bond and be connected to others (in no society on earth are men the primary caretakers).

- Women have more acute senses of smell and greater color perception.

- Men are generally less connected to other people than are women. Women generally ask relevant questions and are more willing to communicate answers than are men.

Knowing how the brain functions of males and females are alike and how they are different is invaluable when planning lessons and organizing activities. This information is especially important when creating grouping activities where communication and sharing skills are so important.

ENGAGE THE BRAIN

The brain is such a complex organism that it needs to be stimulated on multiple planes. Boredom can come quickly when the brain is not engaged in challenging, relevant activities or when few of the senses are engaged. Think about how many times you were driving a car and the routine of a long trip almost mesmerized you into losing awareness of the road. Remember the drive to work that has become so routine and automatic that you fail to notice changes in the landscape. "When did they put that store there?" you ask only to be told that it opened two weeks before.

The brain can process many sources at once. While people think that they do one thing at a time (some teachers actually encourage or enforce this process), this is an illusion, since biologically, physically, intellectually, and emotionally the brain is constantly doing multiprocessing (pick up a penny . . . the brain recognizes it as a penny and utilizes the sensory system to determine density, weight, size, texture, color, shape, hardness, and so on in an instant). The classroom environment (if it's sterile and shows no connection or demonstration of student accomplishments) and presentation at a slower pace with one thing following immediately after the next ad infinitum may actually curtail learning by creating boredom. All students need the stimulation and motivation to proceed toward the goal of the lesson.

STRATEGIES FOR MEANINGFUL LEARNING

The educator can benefit from proven brain-based research using many techniques. The following list contains some strategies that make the learning meaningful and the educational environment positive.

- Use tie-ins or hooks to encourage learners to make personal connections. Relate the new learning to previous experiences, and tie it to what comes next.

- Use techniques that mimic real-world applications and engage the senses.

- Try to create an atmosphere of "relaxed alertness" (the brain is prepared to learn but is in a nonstressful state) that is low in producing threat or fear but is high in challenge and risk taking (Lackney, 2002).

- Let students express their learning style in presenting a product.

- Let them present materials using color and texture so that the classroom environment gives them connection and ownership. Use such things as posters, music, drawings, graphs, and maps to enhance the ability of the brain to engage in multilevels of awareness.

- Make sure cooperative learning projects are mixed gender for maximum effectiveness in communication and understanding.

- Be flexible in creating a system of rules and rewards instead of just rules and punishments.

- Stimulate the student's brain by being a positive, nonthreatening role model.

- Use rote memorization in very limited situations, since it doesn't allow the brain to engage in personalizing the learning.

- Try to create both a time and a place for reflection to occur so students can process the learning, because reflection time is necessary for the brain to process information most thoroughly (Stahl, 1994). Wait after asking a question and after listening to an answer. Give all of the students time to process and adjust to the responses.

- Keep in mind that the whole physiology of the body is engaged in the learning process: Movement and application are crucial to long-term learning since they help to implant an image of doing something for the student. Don't let students sit motionless because you are more concerned about class control than class learning. Make the classroom a place of motion and involvement by changing seating patterns to accommodate the needs of the students and of the lesson.

- Present information so that students use a multimodal approach in learning. The more sensory experiences, the more probability of retention. Students have more pathways to recall the learning.

- Teach the organizational structures present within a subject area so students have hooks to tie in new and prior information.

- Provide links from the classroom to the world outside the classroom so that students can readily tie in what they are learning to where and how they will use the learning.

- Utilize both the resources of the school and those of the community to create a meaningful learning experience. The classroom should be an extension of the educational community, a learning laboratory where ideas can be applied in a safe environment before being tested outside. Technology, interdepartmental collaboration, community and business partnerships, and natural environmental resources all need to be explored and incorporated into the overall scheme of education.

- Create or find places where group learning can take place. Use corridors, school libraries, cafeterias, auditoriums, and so on, which create social learning situations and stimulate the brain.

- Use data to have students address group learning difficulties. Students brainstorm solutions and methods of assessment. Both individual and group accountability increases as students are actively engaged in real-world application and solution.

SAMPLE LESSON

The following math lesson is an example of creating challenge and application. The teacher has provided an opportunity for students to work in a cooperative setting, transfer new information into a prior knowledge base, utilize a multimodal approach to embed knowledge further, and use the knowledge in a real-world application. The students will be physically moving around, brainstorming, self-checking for understanding, and presenting solutions.

Subject: Geometry   Grades: 6–8

Objective/Standard: Students will understand the structure of a right triangle and compute the length of any of the sides by knowing the length of two of the other sides.

Vocabulary: Right triangle, right angle, base, height, hypotenuse, square of a number

Materials Needed: Graph paper, ruler, pen or pencil, scissors, calculator, ladder or board, measuring tape

Lesson Plan: Organize students into groups of four and discuss right triangle, right angle, base, height, hypotenuse, and square of a number. Ask students in each group to use graph paper to make four cutouts of right triangles, each with a different base length. Tell students to measure the sides and hypotenuse of each triangle to the nearest 16th of an inch. Challenge students to work in their groups to discover a relationship between the base and height and the hypotenuse of the triangles. Let them think of all the possible ways of relating the three sides. The students may use calculators to test their suppositions. When the students find the relationship between the two sides and the hypotenuse, have them measure and record the following information on each triangle:

- Measurements of sides *a*, *b*, and hypotenuse *c*
- Computations: squares of *a*, *b*, and *c*
- Relationship observed

Ask students what observations they find and have them check if the figures apply to each of the right triangles. Students should understand that the sum of the squares of each side is equal to the square of the hypotenuse. Tell them that this is known as the *Pythagorean Theorem*.

Real-World Application: Bring a ladder or a board to the classroom and ask students to measure its length. Place the ladder against a wall and measure the distance between the foot of the ladder or board and the wall. Ask students to determine how high on the wall the ladder or board reaches.

Then, tell the students in each group they have two tent poles that are each 7 feet long. Each one will be driven into the ground 2 feet, one at the front and one at the back of the tent. Likewise each group has four pieces of rope 8 feet long, each with a small loop at both ends. Two ropes will be used to attach to each tent pole and to stakes driven into the ground. The front stakes will be 6 feet from each other; the back stakes will be 5 feet from each other. How far does each stake have to be from the respective tent pole?

Assessment: Ask each group of students to come up with a real-world problem that would challenge others to apply the theorem. Share the problems among the groups. Determine the success of the problem according to the following criteria: clarity of expression and requirements, correct use of the theorem, and real-world applicability.

AM I DOING IT RIGHT?

The teacher may use the checklist in Figure 12.1 to see whether the elements of the brain-based classroom are included in daily planning or are afterthoughts. Column 1 shows what needs to be done on a regular basis. Teaching is both a complex art and a science; assessment tools are necessary to keep educators on target.

Since parents are accountable for the health and welfare of the student, they, also, can use a checklist (see Figure 12.2) to make sure they are actively engaged in the student's learning process.

WHAT MOST PEOPLE NEED TO KNOW

When designing curricula to meet the objectives of standards-based learning, middle managers and teachers need to be aware of how a student learns as

Figure 12.1 Teacher Checklist for a Brain-Based Classroom

ELEMENTS OF A BRAIN-BASED CLASSROOM	DONE REGULARLY	DONE SPORADICALLY	NOT DONE
I use straight lecture very infrequently.			
I require a minimum use of rote memorization.			
I engage students both mentally and physically.			
I provide reflection time during the lesson so students can process the information.			
I create an atmosphere free of threat and fear but filled with challenge.			
I encourage respect between teacher and student and student with student.			
I try to create real-world application scenarios.			
I use peripherals (posters, maps, etc.) to stimulate and to reinforce problem solving.			
I try to provide links between new information and prior learning.			
I try to provide regular and timely feedback.			
I try to create situations where the brain may develop patterns involving the learning.			
I try to engage as many student modalities as possible.			
I teach students methods of transferring information.			
I create a physical environment that is conducive to learning.			
I use the whole school environment to engage the students.			

well as what a student is expected to learn. Simply slapping together lessons to match a standard does not ensure success. Even providing well-constructed assessments doesn't complete the process until one factors in the need for students to be challenged and not threatened, to be reinforced in positive ways rather than just to be chided for temporary setbacks, to be encouraged to take creative risks rather than penalized for thinking outside the box. Understanding how the brain functions is important because it becomes another tool that the teacher can use to engage students into the learning and application process.

Figure 12.2   Parent Checklist for Brain-Based Learning

BRAIN-BASED APPLICATION	YES	NO
I emphasize the need for correct amounts of sleep and rest.		
I provide an environment free from threat and undue stress.		
I provide opportunities for my child to apply the learning in real-world problem-solving situations.		
I provide constructive feedback.		
I try to tie my child's learning to previous experiences.		
I encourage positive questioning.		
I am acutely aware of signs of stress and depression.		
I provide reflection time for my child.		
I encourage the use of organizational strategies.		

WHAT SOME PEOPLE NEED TO KNOW

More is probably known about the topography of Mars than is definitive about the complex workings of the human brain. With that in mind, administrators have to keep up with the latest brain research, but should not become involved in the latest brain-based fad. Much valuable research is going on at the moment; hopefully, new insights will produce more information on how the brain learns best and what strategies can promote that learning.

While some facts about brain-based learning have proven to be accurate, additional research is needed to substantiate some of the more recent findings in relationship to education.

School systems, often caught up in the educational fad of the moment as a quick fix, must proceed cautiously and must employ those aspects of brain-based learning that are scientifically researched, tested, and proven beyond question.

SUMMARY

While there are many important aspects of brain-based learning, the following list highlights the crucial areas explored in this chapter:

- The brain operates best in an environment that is free from stress and fear but works well with challenge and creativity.
- Students learn better by doing.

- The brain benefits when learning information in context rather than in isolation.
- The brain tries to make connections and construct patterns to find meaning.
- Rote memorization is not the most effective method of learning.
- Physical movement helps the brain to process new ideas and information.

Reporting Progress 13

On a typical day, the following scenario is enacted in millions of homes:

Parent: What did you do in school today?

Student: Nothing.

The parent, who has put in an entire day of work and usually can't wait to tell everyone how well or how poorly things went that day, is suddenly frustrated by a young person who, through this vague answer, has supposedly completed five to six hours doing "nothing." While this dialogue may seem so typical that it's unimportant, the truth is that it reveals some distinct failures with the traditional assessment, grading, and reporting system. Under the traditional system, the student may have received little meaningful feedback on today's performance, and the parent may be unaware of the goals and expectations the student should be working toward at the moment. To the student, who is in the dark about the significance of the day's lessons, "nothing" may appear to be an appropriate, though inaccurate, answer.

"A grade is an inadequate report of an inaccurate judgment by a biased and variable judge of the extent to which a student has attained an undefined level of mastery of an indefinite amount of material" (Boyle, 1996). While the statement may seem scathing, it had little effect on a system that for a number of years was engrained with letter grades of A, B, C, D, and F. Only recently have school districts examined their assessment and reporting systems and made significant changes to the benefit of all the stakeholders.

Standards-based grading is communicating individual student progress over time upon publicly known learning standards based on an analysis of observable evidence demonstrating the student's ability to apply the knowledge with repeated and consistent success across disciplines. The purpose of grades is to provide students with information that they can use to evaluate and adjust their performance, to serve as indicators of where a student is in the learning spectrum toward achieving a goal (mastery of a standard), to provide data that can be used to evaluate and adjust the effectiveness of the teaching and learning processes, and to communicate to parents both the goals of the learning process as well as a continuum of where their child is on the road to achieving these goals. Knowing this but having an infrequent reporting system based on the vagaries of interpretation by both teacher and student does little to contribute to sustained learning. Quite often, the traditional system actually helps to foster an adversarial relationship among the stakeholders as each one brings a different interpretation to the table. Likewise, in many traditional reporting systems, the parents are left out of the information loop during a time when their involvement, guidance, and motivation may best help the student to succeed.

WHAT EVERYONE NEEDS TO KNOW

Traditional grading systems, while seeming to fulfill the need of providing information and motivation to the student and the teacher, quite often convey confusion and promote unnecessary competition.

Traditional Grading

- The teaching goals and expectations are private.
- Each teacher sets his or her interpretation and value on each test, project, and so on.
- These expectations vary among teachers and are often not clear to parents or students.
- Students, moving from subject to subject on a typical day, generally encounter multiple grading systems.
- Both academics and nonacademics (behavior, effort, attendance, and so on) are grouped together and averaged.
- Students can achieve satisfactory grades even without showing proficiency of the subject matter.
- Assessment is designed from instruction, and tests are often given as tools to keep students on task rather than to ensure that students know, understand, and can apply the knowledge. Most assessment is summative.
- Teachers use variable scales to judge product, so students are often confused about their progress or lack of it at any given time (even teachers have a difficult time to determine a student's level of accomplishment at a specific time).
- Teachers bring in their individual ideas/preferences about student work.
- Students are often measured against an imaginary perfect student ("We'll have to scale the scores because everyone did poorly on the test") or against each other. Individual accomplishment is subject to group achievement (scaling).
- Grade letters are used, which have wide variation in interpretation and application.
  - Most computer programs do not allow the input of an A+ or an F–.
  - In some systems 80–89 is a B while in others 85–92 is a B.

- Criteria for evaluation and scoring often come from the test.

- Students are not given specific goals before the assessment so they are unclear about expectations.

- Students (and often parents) become grade-oriented and lose sight of where the student is on the learning continuum as long as the marks look good.

- Often, teachers use equally weighted assessments (daily homework assignments are often averaged in with reports, essays, and the like). The degree of learning is not measured accurately.

- The present system forces teachers to have "enough grades" each marking term to justify the student's grade at the end of the term.
  - Since the grade is the end measurement goal (rather than the level of learning), teachers want to make sure the record book contains enough marks to justify the student's grade.
  - Teachers do this because they have been taught to do this and because the present system doesn't allow for variance.

A student in his junior year of high school had to write a lengthy research paper. The English department had set a two-month window in which students would work on the project on their own time. Each two-week period, students would be required to turn in one aspect of the work they had completed to date (select a thesis, prepare a preliminary outline, and so on). Students were supposed to receive an ongoing grade for each segment completed with the final grade being an average of the sum of the parts. This student couldn't work in such a structure. He never passed in any of the parts but assured the teacher that he was working. On the day the project was due, he awoke at 4:00 AM in the morning and wrote the entire research paper. The work was brilliant. The teacher gave him an A+ and praised the achievement. The student had conditioned himself to work under his own imposed deadline. In his senior year, he had the department head as his teacher. He received an F on his research paper. The department chair admitted to the previous teacher that the paper was equally brilliant, but the department chair had taken points off because the student had not met the intermediate deadlines, even though both the student and the other teacher had previously informed the department head of the manner in which the student worked. Although the department chair stated that the paper was A+ work, the teacher gave the student an F. The department chair had individualized the grading to get a mark, not to ensure learning.

- Teachers often score first efforts, and feedback comes too late.

- Students often receive a composite score for variable elements within a project. They cannot decipher where they made the most improvement and where they need additional work; the grades are holistic in the sense that they are all inclusive.

- Grades generally are given at the end of a project or a class, after corrections and adjustments can be made (summative assessment).

- Grades are evaluative and often deal with the worthiness of student achievement rather than with the level of achievement.

- Often grades get identified with specific students. They are used to assign students to levels within course offerings and are, many times, the instruments that lock a person into a performance level rather than provide opportunity for growth.

- Specific, easily measurable, identifiable components of a course (such as times tables, chemical symbols, noun-pronoun agreement, dates of the Louisiana Purchase) tend to be the focus of grades, rather than problem-solving, real-world application.

- Instead of showing the student's individual growth, grades are more statistical in showing a student's standing in relationship to a group.

Standards-based grading systems give students opportunities to revise and adjust, two conditions that often provide the necessary motivation for learning.

Standards-Based Grading

- The teaching goals are public.

- Teachers, students, and parents all know the expectations and the measurement criteria to be used to judge the degree of progress and success.

- Academic achievement is separate from behaviors.

- Students, parents, and teachers can see where the student is in relationship to his or her progress involving the subject standards.

- The assessment is designed from the standards.

- All stakeholders know up front the expectations, requirements, and level of performance desired.

- Exemplars of student work are used to provide students with models.

- Students receive specific descriptive feedback to allow them to make ongoing corrections.

- Predetermined scoring criteria known to all students and parents are used to indicate progress.

- Assessments are weighted and are not equal.

- Teachers do not score first efforts.

- Assessments are prescriptive and allow for analysis and adjustment.

- Scores are given per standard.

- Students have a better understanding about where they are in achieving a level of accomplishment on each standard; they are then better able to work harder on areas of concern.

- Assessment grading allows students to see improvement over time, while the work is in progress and corrections can be made.

- Because it focuses on learning and takes into consideration all of the variables (e.g., teaching style, time on task, background knowledge), assessment grading is not judgmental.

- Assessments tend to be private since the student is not being measured against any other student.

- The focus is on individual student improvement rather than on the student's grade relationship to the group, so assessments are almost always distributed in an anonymous fashion.

- A student who is weak in one standard may excel in another.

- Assessment looks at specific parts of the learning spectrum so that correction and adjustment can be made.

- Assessment deals more with thinking skills and problem-solving applications to real-world settings.

Traditional grading is often based on an imprecise set of criteria that is developed from the task; therefore, students usually find themselves working in the dark as to the expectations of a project. There is no real consistency from teacher to teacher, even on the same assignment. Often students approach another teacher to read a piece of writing and ask what that teacher would give as a mark. The new teacher usually refuses, tactfully, not wanting to get involved in a grading controversy with a colleague. This happens frequently, which is further proof that the traditional methods of evaluation are so variable that they tend to be more confusing than they are clarifying. Sometimes even teachers aren't sure what they are looking for, so how can students fill an expectation that hasn't been clearly identified? The project in question becomes focused on a grade rather than on a level of understanding and applicability. The grade becomes an end to learning rather than a means to progressing.

WHAT MOST PEOPLE NEED TO KNOW

The need for assessments immediately creates the need for a reporting system that conveys the necessary information and data in a clear, precise, and usable manner to all of the stakeholders. Traditional grading and reporting systems must be revamped and made to correspond to the standards-based model.

- Content standards have to be established first.
- Rubrics and other assessment devices must be clear and specific; they must be developed across grade levels.
  - o There must be an ease of applying them and in using the results to make informed decisions.
  - o When students are involved in creating assessments, the results are usually immediate and produce positive results.
- Performance objectives and assessments should be tied to the standards and must be consistent across the grade level.

- Traditional grading and reporting systems must be revamped and made to correspond to the standards-based needs.

- Parents are an integral factor in the education process and must be accessed and kept involved. Communication lines need to be kept open constantly to update parents as to the progress of the students so that correction can be made as early as possible, and parents can assist the teacher.

- Assessment should focus on real-world application and problem solving.

- Data collection and analysis are essential to ongoing improvement.

- Teachers need to be instructed in how to collect and interpret data, to share data with the other stakeholders, and to use data to drive decision making by the teacher and the students.

- On standards-based report cards, subjects are listed by name (mathematics, English language arts, and so on) but are defined by the content standard being covered in that subject (such as vocabulary, fractions, weather).
   - In this way, focus is always being kept on the standard rather than on the traditional teacher-selected, textbook-driven approach that may or may not cover the standard.
   - The curriculum (what is taught), the method (how knowledge is taught), and the evaluation are all tied directly to the standards that the student must master.

- Teachers must be given professional development using outside consultants, in-house master practitioners, textual resources, and the like. They need training.

- As with students, teachers need to have a reason to adopt the standards-based assessment and grading procedures, to see the overall objective, and to know the steps necessary to arrive at the goal.

- Teachers need support from mentors, curriculum coordinators and facilitators, team leaders, department chairs, and administrators.

- They, likewise, require immediate and frequent feedback so that they can self-correct and adjust.

The traditional grading system is full of inconsistencies in how teachers arrive at a student's grade. Some skew the content mastery by whitewashing it with a student's effort: "Jack was trying so hard that I gave him the benefit of the doubt." "I know she can do better." "I figure if I give him a good grade, he'll work harder in the future." Other teachers don't cover all of the standards, while still others continue to make the classroom environment into a "top dog" competition with students attaining grades not so much by what they have learned but more by how they stack up to other learners. Often, parents, who had to deal with the inconsistencies of the traditional grading and reporting system when they went to school, are unwilling to go to another form of reporting that they don't clearly understand. Parents feel they "learned to play the game" as students and expect that tradition to carry on. They often want only a bottom-line report of their child's performance because that's all their parents got about them. And the traditional report card is a compact piece of paper that doesn't require much reading or much thought process. Nor does it require parents to get too involved if they choose not to do so.

Then, what are the advantages of a standards-based reporting system? First, the standards that the student is expected to master are clearly spelled out. No longer is English language arts listed. Now, the entire category of verbal, writing, listening, analyzing, interpreting, criticizing, and presenting skills is covered. Parents and students can see specifically where greater emphasis needs to be placed. Decoding, vocabulary, structure, comprehension, organization, and mechanics are all included, and the student knows what aspects have been learned and which ones need more concentration and focus. And measuring, converting, multiplying, classifying, squaring, and factoring skills replace mathematics as a catchall title. Second, students are not measured against other students but against their own mastery of the standards, and they can see where they are on the performance continuum: below grade-level standard, approaching grade-level standard, at grade-level standard, or advanced grade-level standard. Third, all teachers cover the same standards and use the same assessment pieces to measure student performance. The standards are weighed consistently and nonjudgmentally across the grade levels. And the standards are the key element of the report card; enrichment is detailed differently (see Figure 13.1).

The standards-based report card is actually a detailed summary of collected data in which teachers communicate and students and parents learn what

Figure 13.1   Traditional Versus Standards-Based Report Cards

TRADITIONAL REPORT CARD	*STANDARDS-BASED REPORT CARD*
Small, compact, usually pocket-sized, with grades on one side	Larger, multipaged or two-sided
General subject designations (mathematics, science, and so on)	Subject designations are broken down into their component parts (English language arts = reading, writing, language conventions, listening and speaking). Each of these have subcategories, such as decoding, fluency, literary response, analysis
Letter grades with number interpretations corresponding to totals from the grade book	Numbers correspond to levels of success (below standard to advanced)
Subjective (using emotional judgment, inconsistent assessment tools, student vs. student environment, often weighted scores)	Objective (based on the standards and assessments, and individual progress)
Feedback too general to focus on specific areas of concern or accomplishment	Feedback is specific
Provides vague data to make adjustment in student performance	Provides specific data to make adjustment in student performance
Enrichment included as part of the complete subject grade without specifying under which category or subcategory the enrichment occurred	A separate enrichment category; affects only the category or subcategory in which it occurs

corrections and adjustments need to be made to achieve mastery of the standards. The traditional report card form is too condensed and too general to provide the necessary information for sound decision making.

As an example, take building a home. Generally, people begin by purchasing a lot, making considerations about location; availability of city services; access to schools, shopping, and work; and price. Then people look for housing types that would fit their needs, budget, and the lot size. Narrowing down their selection, they then need to secure a loan, get a contractor, collect numerous pieces of data (such as lenders, mortgage rates, interior layout) before making the multiple decisions that will result in a home being built. Everyone wants a complete picture, a total breakdown of all of the offerings and the prices before going ahead.

A standards-based report card offers more data on which to make important decisions. It clearly shows areas where students may move on to enrichment activities, in which they don't do more work but do apply what they have learned to new problem-solving situations using higher-order thinking skills. In addition, it also shows where students need more review. The report card gives teachers, students, and parents a snapshot of what the proficient student looks like and can do, as well as where the student is in relationship to accomplishing these ends. It allows parents to see the areas of progress and concern, and enlists them into the search for solutions. The teacher now knows where to put the focus on reviewing, reteaching, or enriching. Parents know that although their child has met the standards, they are aware of "to what degree" and how the student develops higher-order thinking skills by using the standards in multiple contexts. The checklist in Figure 13.2 shows what criteria a standards-based report card needs to have to be a functional tool.

A standards-based report card can't be dropped on teachers, students, or parents overnight. There are plans to be made and obstacles to be overcome before the card can be implemented (see Figure 13.3).

A standards-based report card helps students and parents to understand that learning is a process done in stages. The card reports the student's progress in meeting the performance objectives that demonstrate that the student has understood and mastered the standard. It also shows that actual learning has taken place and can be documented. Likewise, it provides the data necessary for teachers to make solid decisions on whether to focus their efforts on reteaching or reviewing.

WHAT SOME PEOPLE NEED TO KNOW

Instituting a new reporting system can be a complex process, unless there is involvement by representatives of all of the stakeholders. Since the results (a new report card) will affect and increase the lines of communication, modeling an open dialogue on establishing the process of change is an excellent place to start. This course of action must not be begun until teachers and administrators have been trained in all aspects of the standards-based model and are implementing these strategies. Administrators must ensure that this is happening at all levels.

Administrators need to convene a committee of middle managers, teachers, parents, and students to study models of reporting standards-based data to

Figure 13.2 Standards-Based Report Card Criteria

REQUIREMENTS	MET
1. Four categories: beginning, meeting grade level, proficient, advanced (other comparable terms are also used).	
2. Numerical designations corresponding to the four categories: 1, 2, 3, 4.	
3. General subjects (e.g., mathematics, science), their component parts (e.g., number sense, measurement), subcategories under the component parts (e.g., problem solving, factoring).	
4. The scope and sequence broken up by semesters (prescribed periods) so students and parents know where the students are in relationship to the standards being covered.	
5. An explanation of each of the terms and standards (this may be found in the introductory page or on the back of the grading sheet).	
6. If possible, a continuum scale to indicate where a student is in progress from beginning a standard through the mastery stage. This feature does not lock teachers into categories that may be too tight (simply using four numbers) and gives parents and students an opportunity to see where the students actually are toward completion of the standard. Example: Beginning · · · At Grade Level · · · Proficient · · · Advanced **Factoring** 1 2 3 4 Beginning · · · At Grade Level · · · Proficient · · · Advanced **Measuring** 1 2 3 4 If the continuum line is present, an example needs to be included, filled out, and interpreted for both students and parents.	
7. A narrative box should be included for each subject area. The narrative can include levels of enrichment for those students who have mastered the standard or advice for students who are still working toward meeting the standard. This is an important feature because it allows parents to see that the student is both excelling and is actively engaged in the classroom.	

Figure 13.3 Addressing Potential Problems and Providing Solutions

POTENTIAL PROBLEMS	POSSIBLE SOLUTIONS
Parents object and want the simplified report card they used.	Before introducing the card, an extensive parent information campaign should be mounted to include the following: ❑ Whole school meetings ❑ Grade-level meetings ❑ School council newsletters ❑ Models (card sent home with interpreted results) ❑ Parent brochures ❑ Student training ❑ Press coverage ❑ Web site postings ❑ School newspaper ❑ Parents night presentations Parents are more inclined to go along with something they understand.
Teachers object saying the process of filling out the report card is too time-consuming.	Many software programs can solve these time problems. The traditional grade book creates problems since it is designed to accommodate letter or number grades only. Districts can create their own grade books (pages easily secured in three-ring binders). These tools can be attuned to the standards and the assessment forms, and can be designed to give an ongoing representation of a student's progress that would be easily translatable into report card form.

the stakeholders, including both the standards-based report card and the standards-based mark book.

- Once adoption of a format is made, an all-out information campaign has to be organized to instruct teachers, parents, and students on the information contained within the card.

- Professional development and specialized training must be offered to teachers to use the new data collection and reporting formats.

EASY . . . EASIER . . . EASIEST IN GRADING SYSTEMS

Three of the arguments that are often heard from teachers are as follows:

- "We don't make the policy. That's handed down to us. We have no control over the grading system."

- "Look, nobody ever taught me about mark books and grading. I picked up bits and pieces over the years. My system works, for me."

- "I use grading software. It takes all this stuff into account and averages my grades for me. It's easier."

First, teachers are the grading system. Their input has to be the most respected since they are directly involved with the stakeholders. Their voice must be heard, so teachers must make their needs known to all of the administrators, through superintendent and school committee. A system that attempts change without hearing the needs of the teachers and soliciting their input is doomed to mediocrity.

Second, while many teachers were given a grade book, along with a room key and other supplies, when they began teaching, they really weren't instructed in its use. They had to figure out a system for compiling grades that supposedly worked. Only when the marks were challenged due to a parental request did the teacher have to expose this grade book to any public scrutiny. Rarely did teachers get together with each other to show their books to each other and discuss ways for improving their reporting systems. So, what they have often isn't really a grading system but more a jerry-rigged device that acts more as a diary than as an instrument that provides data to be used in monitoring and adjusting.

Third, there are many types of software or Web-based grading programs. Some do only the numeric calculations rather than showing progress on a continuum scale involving the standards. Teachers need an ongoing system that lets teacher, student, and parent know where the student is on the continuum scale toward developing proficiency and mastery of the standard. Programs such as MMS, CompassLearning, Gradebook2, WebGrade, and GradeQuick all provide a way to record grades using standards-based assessment as the key. Some of these programs even provide online communication with parents so that a true educational community can exist.

SUMMARY

Standards-based report cards are a logical step toward providing critical and timely information to the principal educational stakeholders. Although they are often the last step considered in changing over to a standards-based system, they are, nonetheless, a vital one and should neither be overlooked nor put off too long.

- Standards-based assessment systems provide a clearer, more precise picture of what a student knows and can do.

- Standards-based report cards provide the necessary data for teachers and students to adjust and focus the learning.

- Standards-based report cards provide more necessary information for parents to become active members of the school community.

Glossary

ACCOUNTABILITY is accepting responsibility to ensure the successful completion of an act in an appropriate time frame (it's doing my job as a teacher or an administrator; it's accepting my role as a student or parent).

ANNUAL SCHOOL REPORT CARD is a report that is mandated by the state that documents the academic performance of students (they're checking to see that I'm doing my job as a teacher or administrator).

APPLICATION is using learned knowledge and skills to do something measurable and visible that demonstrates their effective use (using what I, the student, learned successfully).

ASSESSMENT is measuring the level or degree to which something is accomplished (how well am I, the student, doing?).

CURRICULUM is all courses offered by a school; everything a teacher is supposed to do; often mistakenly interpreted as the list of texts that make up the scope and sequence of the lessons (a catch-all word).

DATA is factual evidence of the degree to which something has been learned and applied (for example, 96% of all students got problem 6 correct on the final exam; facts).

DIFFERENTIATION is addressing individual needs involving rate and degree of learning and providing opportunities to apply knowledge and skills at different levels of accomplishment (giving me, the student, a chance to learn, practice, and advance at my own rate).

FORMATIVE ASSESSMENT is an ongoing evaluation of the degree of accomplishment of an objective; during the process, feedback is provided to promote correction and adjustment (lets me see where I, the student, am and what I can do to improve now).

GRADE-LEVEL EXPECTATIONS are what students are expected to know and be able to do in each academic discipline at a specific grade level (what I, the student, should know and be able to do at this grade level).

GROUPING is placing students with their peers in various combinations to promote decision making and to increase interactive learning opportunities (teaching me, the student, how to learn and use my skills in real world type interactions).

LEARNING MODALITIES are the styles (visual, auditory, or motor) that learners use to concentrate on, process, and retain information (how I, the student, learn).

PATTERNING is the brain searching for meaningful organization and categorization of information, tying what is being learned to what has already been learned (making connections).

PERFORMANCE ASSESSMENT is a tool that allows students to see how they are doing using a predetermined scale of success (I, the student, see how I am doing so I can make corrections).

PERFORMANCE OBJECTIVE is what a teacher wants the students to be able to do to demonstrate they have learned the knowledge and skills and can use them successfully (what I, the student, have to do to show I've learned something).

RUBRIC is a scoring grid with required performance criteria and degrees of success (an easy way to tell how I'm doing now).

SCAFFOLDING is providing temporary support for a student, during which time the teacher models a skill and then slowly shifts responsibility to the student to apply the skill (teacher helps me until I can do it myself).

SKILLS are the ability to perform the specific steps of an activity successfully (I, as a student, follow a series of steps to find the logical conclusion).

STANDARD is an educationally and socially accepted level of accomplishment that equates with success (what society feels I need to know to succeed).

STRENGTHS are the ability to perform a specific task repeatedly over time with near perfect execution (doing it right more than once).

SUMMATIVE ASSESSMENTS are exams or tests that are given at the end of a unit of learning (I either know it or . . .).

WALKTHROUGH is a short observation when a peer or administrator checks for an element from the standards-based model being used in the classroom (let me see that you're doing it).

References

Boyle, B., & Christie, T. (1996). *Issues in setting standards.* London: Falmer. Retrieved February 21, 2005, from http://www.unf.edu/dept/cirt/workshops/ElderAssessment1

Dale, E. (1969). *Audiovisual methods in teaching* (3rd ed.). New York: Dryden.

Denzin, P. (1997). *Drivetrain sequence of the standards-based school* and *Drivetrain sequence of the traditional school.* Retrieved August 19, 2004, from http://www.cde .state.co.us/action/standards/pdf/drivet.pdf#search

Golding, W. (1954). *Lord of the flies.* New York: Pedigree.

Hannaford, C. (1995). *Smart moves.* Alexandria, VA: Great Ocean. Retrieved December 15, 2004, from http://esl.about.com/library/lessons/blbraingym.htm

Hersey, J. (1960). *The child buyer.* New York: Bantam.

James, A. N. (2007). *Teaching the male brain: How boys think, feel, and learn in school* (3rd ed.). Thousand Oaks, CA: Corwin Press.

Jensen, E. (1998). *Teaching with the brain in mind.* Alexandria, VA: Association for Supervision and Curriculum Development.

Jerald, C. (2003). "Cooking with data" to reduce achievement gaps. *ENC Focus, 10*(1), 24–28.

Lackney, J. (2002). *12 design principles based on brain-based learning principles.* Retrieved November 20, 2004, from http://www.designshare.com/Research/BrainBased Learn98.htm

Montgomery, S. M. (1995). *Addressing diverse learning styles through the use of multimedia.* Presented at ASEE/IEE Frontiers in Education, session 3a2–Multimedia. Retrieved January 2, 2005, from http://fie.engrng.pitt.edu/fie95/3a2/3a22/3a22.htm

Orwell, G. (1949). *1984.* New York: Signet Classic.

Stahl, R. J. (1994). *Using "think-time" and "wait-time" skillfully in the classroom.* Bloomington, IN: Social Science Education. (ERIC Document Reproduction Service No. ED 370885). Retrieved January 25, 2005, from http://atozteacherstuff.com/ pages/1884.shtml

Theroux, P. (2004). *Differentiating instruction.* Retrieved November 20, 2004, from http://members.shaw.ca/priscillatheroux/differentiation.htm

Weiss, R. P. (2001). *The mind-body connection in learning.* American Society for Training and Development. Retrieved January 20, 2005, from www.trans4mind.com/ news/mind-body.html

Index

CORWIN PRESS

The Corwin Press logo—a raven striding across an open book—represents the union of courage and learning. Corwin Press is committed to improving education for all learners by publishing books and other professional development resources for those serving the field of PreK–12 education. By providing practical, hands-on materials, Corwin Press continues to carry out the promise of its motto: **"Helping Educators Do Their Work Better."**